AIRCRAFT ACCIDENT REPORT 1/96

CW00322472

Air A   Branch

Department of Transport

Report on the accident to
Boeing 737-2D6C, 7T-VEE
at Willenhall, Coventry, Warwickshire
on 21 December 1994

This investigation was carried out in accordance with
The Civil Aviation (Investigation of Air Accidents) Regulations 1989

London: HMSO

LIST OF RECENT AIRCRAFT ACCIDENT AND INCIDENT REPORTS
ISSUED BY AIR ACCIDENTS INVESTIGATION BRANCH

These Reports are available from HMSO Bookshops and Accredited Agents

Department of Transport
Air Accidents Investigation Branch
Defence Research Agency
Farnborough
Hampshire GU14 6TD

7 December 1995

The Right Honourable Sir George Young
Secretary of State for Transport

Sir,

I have the honour to submit the report by Mr R StJ Whidborne, an Inspector of Air Accidents, on the circumstances of the accident to Boeing 737-2D6C, 7T-VEE, near Willenhall, Coventry on 21 December 1994.

I have the honour to be
Sir
Your obedient servant

K P R Smart
Chief Inspector of Air Accidents

Contents

Contents (continued)

5   Appendices

Appendix A   Boeing approach procedures
Appendix B   METAR and RVR logs
Appendix C   Special meteorological observation criteria
Appendix D   Coventry radar vectoring area (D-1)
                 Coventry SRA Runway 23 chart (D-2)
                 Coventry AIP RAC SRA data page (D-3)
Appendix E   Meteorological observer training AIC
Appendix F   Extracts from CVR transcript
Appendix G   Analysis of impact between aircraft and tower, and subsequent flight path
Appendix H   Photographs showing approach to Runway 23
Appendix J   7T-VEE flight operations
Appendix K   Public Safety Zones
Appendix L   UK airports, met observation periods, broadcast facilities, movements and PSZ status
Appendix M   Permits to operate flights and aerodrome operating minima notification requirements
Appendix N   Jeppesen Coventry aerodrome chart and SRA minima page
Appendix P   Aerodrome Operating Minima (AOM) requirements
Appendix R   Aircraft checklist extracts and altimeter checking procedures
Appendix S   Final flight position/height graph (S-1)
                 Final SRA glidepath graph (S-2)
                 Previous approaches during final duty graph (S-3)
Appendix T   Previous approaches made by 7T-VEE
Appendix U   Standard MATS Part 1 phraseology

GLOSSARY OF ABBREVIATIONS USED IN THIS REPORT

AAIB	Air Accidents Investigation Branch	IATA	International Air Transport Association
ADF	Automatic Direction Finder	ICAO	International Civil Aviation Organization
ADI	Attitude Director Indicator		
agl	above ground level	IFR	Instrument Flight Rules
AIC	Aeronautical Information Circular	IGV	Inlet Guide Vane
		ILS	Instrument Landing System
AIP	Aeronautical Information Publication	LATCC	London Air Traffic Control Centre
AIS	Aeronautical Information Service	LOFT	Line-orientated flight training
		MAPt	Missed Approach Point
amsl	above mean sea level	MATS	Manual of Air Traffic Services
ANO	Air Navigation Order	MDA	Minimum Descent Altitude
AOC	Air Operator's Certificate	MDH	Minimum Descent Height
AOM	Aerodrome Operating Minima	MEHT	Minimum Height over Threshold
ASI	Airspeed Indicator		
ATC (O)	Air Traffic Control (Officer)	METAR	Aviation Routine Weather Report
ATIS	Automatic Terminal Information Service		
		MHz	Megahertz
ATPL	Airline Transport Pilot's Licence	MMEL	Master Minimum Equipment List
ATSA	Air Traffic Services Assistant	MTOW	Maximum Take-Off Weight
ATSU	Air Traffic Services Unit	NDB	Non-Directional Beacon
CAA	Civil Aviation Authority	OCH	Obstacle Clearance Height
CAP	Civil Aviation Publication	PAPI	Precision Approach Path Indicator
CCTV	Closed Circuit Television		
C of A	Certificate of Airworthiness	PSZ	Public Safety Zone
CRM	Crew Resource Management	QFE	Height above airfield datum
CVR	Cockpit Voice Recorder	QNH	Corrected mean sea level pressure
DH	Decision Height		
DME	Distance Measuring Equipment	QRH	Quick Reference Handbook
DOT	Department of Transport	RA	Radio Altimeter
DRA	Defence Research Agency	RMI	Radio Magnetic Indicator
FAA	Federal Aviation Administration	RT	Radio Telephony
FD	Flight Director	RTR	Radar Termination Range
FDR	Flight Data Recorder	RVR	Runway Visual Range
FL	Flight Level	SRA	Surveillance Radar Approach
FSM	Flight Safety Management	SRE	Surveillance radar element
FTL	Flight Time Limitation	TAF	Terminal Aerodrome Forecast
GPWS	Ground Proximity Warning System	UHF	Ultra High Frequency
		UTC	Co-ordinated Universal Time
GS	Glideslope	VCR	Visual Control Room
HSI	Horizontal Situation Indicator	VHF	Very High Frequency
IA	International Aviation Directorate	VOR	VHF omnidirectional radio range
IAS	Indicated Airspeed	V_{REF}	Reference threshold speed

Air Accidents Investigation Branch

Aircraft Accident Report No: 1/96 (EW/C94/12/4)

Registered Owner and Operator:	Compagnie Nationale de Transport Aériens, Air Algerie
Aircraft Type and Model:	Boeing 737-2D6C
Nationality:	Algerian
Registration:	7T-VEE
Place of accident:	Willenhall, Coventry, Warwickshire
	Latitude: 52° 23' 13" North
	Longitude: 001° 27' West
Date and Time:	21 December 1994 at 0952 hrs
	All times in this report are UTC

Synopsis

The accident was notified to the Air Accidents Investigation Branch (AAIB) at 1020 hrs on 21 December 1994, and an investigation commenced immediately. The AAIB team consisted of Mr R St J Whidborne (Investigator in Charge), Mr P D Gilmartin (Operations), Mr P N Giles (Operations), Mr C I Coghill (Engineering), Mr S W Moss (Engineering), Mr C A Protheroe (Engineering), Mr S R Culling (Engineering), and Ms A Evans (Flight Recorders). Additionally, accredited representatives of the State of Registry/Operator and the State of Manufacture were appointed to the investigation in accordance with Annex 13 to the Convention on International Civil Aviation.

The accident occurred when the aircraft, which had been chartered for the export of live animals to the Continent, was making a Surveillance Radar Approach (SRA) to Runway 23 at Coventry Airport in conditions of patchy lifting fog. The aircraft descended below the

Minimum Descent Height (MDH) for the approach procedure, and collided with electricity cables and a transmission tower (pylon) which was situated on the extended centreline of the runway, some 1.1 miles from its threshold. The collision caused major damage to the inboard high lift devices on the left wing, and to the left engine. The consequent loss of lift on the left wing, and the thrust asymmetry, caused the aircraft to roll uncontrollably to the left. When passing through a wings vertical attitude, the left wingtip impacted the gable end of a house, causing major structural damage to the property. The aircraft continued rolling to an inverted attitude and impacted the ground in an area of woodland close to the edge of the housing conurbation. An intense fire ensued, during which a large part of the forward fuselage aft to the wheel well, including the wing centre section and the inboard portions of the wings were consumed. The five occupants suffered fatal multiple injuries on impact. There were no injuries to other persons.

The report identifies the following causal factors:

i)   The flight crew allowed the aircraft to descend significantly below the normal approach glidepath during a Surveillance Radar Approach to Runway 23 at Coventry Airport, in conditions of patchy lifting fog. The descent was continued below the promulgated Minimum Descent Height without the appropriate visual reference to the approach lighting or the runway threshold.

ii) The standard company operating procedure of cross-checking altimeter height indications during the approach was not observed and the appropriate Minimum Descent Height was not called by the non handling pilot.

iii) The performance of the flight crew was impaired by the effects of tiredness, having completed over 10 hours of flight duty through the night, during five flight sectors which included a total of six approaches to land.

Nine safety recommendations have been made.

1   Factual Information

1.1   History of the flight

1.1.1   General

The aircraft was owned and operated by Air Algerie, and had been leased by Phoenix Aviation[1] in order to operate a series of live animal export flights from the UK to airports in France and in the Netherlands.

The pilots involved in the accident arrived in the UK on Sunday 18 December 1994. They travelled as passengers on the afternoon scheduled Air Algerie flight into London Heathrow Airport from Algiers and were transported by road to the crew hotel near Coventry Airport.

The accident crew attended a Monday morning briefing session at their hotel, then operated the planned 1230 and 1630 hrs outbound flights from Coventry to Rennes (France). The actual departure times achieved were 1325 and 1729 hrs respectively. The weather conditions were good at Coventry that day, and the crew completed their duty at about 2030 hrs that evening. They were then off duty until the following night, a break in excess of 27 hours.

During their next duty, it was planned to operate two round trips to Amsterdam (Netherlands), with the initial departure at 0030 hrs on 21 December, and final arrival back at Coventry at 0730 hrs. The crew was collected from the hotel 45 minutes before the planned departure time. The flight was delayed a little by the loading, and the aircraft departed with a cargo of livestock at 0059 hrs from Runway 23. The commander was making the radio transmissions while the aircraft was airborne on this flight. It is normal practice for the non-handling pilot to make the radio transmissions while airborne, indicating that the first officer was the handling pilot for the sector.

The aircraft returned empty, again with the first officer as handling pilot. The approach made to Coventry on that occasion was an SRA to Runway 23, initially terminating at 2 miles[2] from touchdown, although as the aircraft approached that range the controller advised that he would continue the approach talkdown to a range of 1 mile. The surface wind was calm, and the visibility was in excess of

---

[1]   Section 1.17 deals with management and organisation aspects.

[2]   Throughout this report 'miles' are nautical miles.

20 km, with scattered cloudbase 4,500 feet. The commander reported that he had the runway in sight when the aircraft was just inside 2 miles from touchdown, and the aircraft landed uneventfully at 0342 hrs. The weather report for that approach had been passed to the crew while they were also in contact with the en route area control. It was not updated or reiterated when the aircraft was transferred to Coventry Approach Radar control.

After arrival, the aircraft was loaded with a further cargo of livestock. With the same crew, it departed again at 0452 hrs. On this sector, the commander was the handling pilot, and the aircraft arrived after an uneventful Instrument Landing System (ILS, frequency 109.5 MHz) approach to Amsterdam's Runway 19R at 0551 hrs. The weather conditions at Amsterdam were good throughout the night. The cargo was unloaded and the aircraft was refuelled with 6,980 litres of Jet A-1 fuel prior to the return flight to Coventry. On board for this flight were the two pilots, an Air Algerie maintenance engineer and two stock handlers employed by Phoenix Aviation.

In accordance with the standard refuelling plan of the operator, sufficient fuel was uplifted to enable the aircraft to fly to Coventry, and then to undertake its next planned flight to Rennes with a fresh flight crew, but without further refuelling. The quantity on board at the time of departure from Amsterdam was 10,500 kg and the estimated fuel used for the flight to Coventry was 2,400 kg.

The forecast Coventry weather that would have been available to the crew while on the ground at Amsterdam was the 0400 to 1300 hrs Terminal Aerodrome Forecast (TAF), which indicated that a visibility of 800 metres in fog was likely to occur between 0400 and 0900 hrs.

The flight departed from Amsterdam at 0642 hrs. Between 0500 and 0600 hrs, the weather at Coventry had deteriorated. Visibility had reduced from over 20 km to 3,500 metres by 0550 hrs, and by 0620 hrs it had reduced further to 800 metres. All of the airfield radio navigation aids were serviceable, but the aircraft was not able to receive the Coventry Runway 23 ILS on frequency 109.75 MHz, as its dual navigation receiver system was not to an updated 40 channel ILS standard (see paragraph 1.8.2.2).

1.1.2   Diversion to East Midlands Airport

On handover from London ATCC, the Coventry Approach Radar controller offered the aircraft radar vectoring for an SRA to Runway 23, terminating at 0.5 miles from touchdown. The crew was then informed that the Runway Visual

Range (RVR) for Runway 23 was 700 metres[3], but the full weather report was not passed, as it had been given to the crew during an earlier radio call. The first officer acknowledged the RVR information, which again suggested that the commander was the handling pilot for the sector. The radar guidance was completed at 0739 hrs, with the aircraft at 0.5 miles from touchdown. The commander had decided to discontinue that approach and executed a go-around[4]. The aircraft was given radar vectors and then cleared to the Coventry Non-Directional Beacon (NDB) in order to take up the holding pattern, which was commenced at 0744 hrs.

Some nine minutes were spent in the holding pattern, during which time the RVR for Runway 23 reduced to 600 metres. The actual weather reports for Birmingham and East Midlands Airports were passed to the crew by Coventry ATC. Birmingham had a visibility of 600 metres with a touchdown RVR for Runway 33 of greater than 1,500 metres, and East Midlands had a visibility of 3,500 metres, with scattered cloudbase 6,000 feet. The crew stated that their intention was to remain in the holding pattern until 0800 hrs awaiting any improvement in the Coventry weather, after which time they would divert to East Midlands. However, at 0749 hrs a message was passed from Phoenix Aviation advising the aircraft to divert to East Midlands Airport and to wait on the ground for a weather improvement.

At 0750 hrs the crew was instructed to remain in the holding pattern at the 'CT' beacon, awaiting co-ordination of an ATC clearance with Birmingham and East Midlands. This instruction was repeated as the crew sought confirmation of it. However, at 0753 hrs, the aircraft was observed on radar to have turned right and was leaving the holding pattern turning towards East Midlands. This caused a potential conflict with traffic inbound to Birmingham, but it was quickly resolved by the Birmingham and Coventry Radar controllers, both of whom filed CAA Occurrence Reports regarding the event.

The aircraft was routed directly towards East Midlands Airport. At 0758 hrs, the crew was offered radar vectoring for an ILS approach to Runway 27. The East Midlands Approach controller queried whether the crew had the frequency of the ILS, and confirmed that it was 109.35 MHz. The commander had taken over the radio transmissions for the handover to East Midlands Approach, and he stated

---

3   The minimum RVR acceptable for the start of an approach under UK criteria was 1,100 metres.

4   See Appendix P with regard to Aerodrome Operating Minima requirements.

that they had tuned the ILS frequency but could not receive it "for the moment" and would advise when they "got the indication". On being passed a closing radar heading for the ILS Localiser, the commander reported that the aircraft ILS was not operating and that the runway was in sight, while still some 8.5 miles from touchdown. The aircraft was re-cleared for a visual approach and transferred to the Aerodrome controller. The first officer again took over the radio transmissions, suggesting that the commander was the handling pilot, and the aircraft landed uneventfully at 0808 hrs.

A handling company at East Midlands was contacted by Phoenix Aviation, who advised that the aircraft must wait there until the Coventry weather improved, as it was not possible to transfer the outbound load from Coventry. The agent was requested to provide the aircraft with the required services, and to arrange breakfast for the crew. All of the occupants, except for the engineer, took advantage of this arrangement by visiting the airport restaurant. No further refuelling or change of loading took place at East Midlands, and no aircraft technical documentation was deposited prior to the next flight.

1.1.3   East Midlands to Coventry sector

At about 0900 hrs, a Phoenix Aviation representative at Coventry Airport observed that the weather appeared to be improving. A call was made to the Air Traffic Services Unit (ATSU) at Coventry, where the Air Traffic Services Assistant (ATSA) was reported to have given an assessment of the current observed weather conditions. The commander was then passed a message from Phoenix Aviation, via the handling agent, indicating that the visibility at Coventry had improved to 1,200 metres with an overcast cloudbase at 600 feet.

The commander contacted Phoenix Aviation by telephone to confirm the message, and decided to undertake the return sector to Coventry. Engines were started at 0927 hrs and the aircraft took off from Runway 27 at 0938 hrs. It was cleared initially to maintain runway heading, climbing to Flight Level (FL) 40[5]. About 40 seconds after takeoff, it was cleared to turn left on a direct track towards the 'CT' NDB and transferred from Aerodrome to Approach control. After about one minute under the control of the East Midlands Approach controller, the aircraft was transferred to Birmingham Approach control.

---

[5]   Flight Level is an altimeter indication obtained with a standard subscale pressure setting of 1013 mb.

The crew was requested to change the transponder squawk, then advised that the aircraft was identified on radar and told they would be offered radar vectors for Runway 23 at Coventry, but were then cleared direct towards the 'CT' beacon to maintain FL40. The crew asked for descent clearance and, after telephone contact between the Birmingham and Coventry ATC units, the aircraft was requested to turn left onto a heading of 110°. It was initially cleared to descend to 2,500 feet on the QNH[6] of 1022 mb. After being under the control of Birmingham for about three minutes, it was handed over to the Coventry Approach Radar controller at 0944 hrs.

The crew was advised that the aircraft was identified on (primary) radar by the Coventry controller, and that it would be positioned by radar vectors for an ILS approach to Runway 23. A heading change onto 090° was instructed. The crew was then advised, in a single transmission, to set the QFE of 1013 mb and descend to maintain height 1,500 feet and to turn left heading 030°. The commander read back the height and pressure setting correctly, but misread the heading as 080°. This was amended by the controller to be 010°, but at this stage the commander replied with a **right** turn to 010°. The controller did not query the readback regarding the incorrect direction of turn because initially the aircraft was observed to start a left turn.

1.1.4   Final SRA to Coventry

The crew was advised that the radar vectors would take the aircraft through the final approach track "for spacing". The controller enquired as to whether the crew was able to carry out an ILS approach, or if an SRA was required. The commander queried the meaning of this transmission, but the question remained unresolved. Because of the position and heading of the aircraft at that time, the controller was concerned that it was about to leave the radar vectoring area in which 1,500 feet was a safe height, and also because of possible confliction with other (unidentified) traffic outside the area. The crew was therefore requested to turn left immediately onto a heading of 010° (a repeat of the previous heading instruction). The commander responded that the aircraft was currently heading 010°, but the controller informed him that the aircraft was in fact tracking 100° and reiterated the left turn request.

---

[6]   An altimeter with its subscale set to QNH pressure indicates Altitude above mean sea level (amsl), and when set to QFE pressure indicates Height above the appropriate QFE datum point, usually a runway threshold or aerodrome reference point.

The controller requested that this turn be continued onto a heading of 260°, which was correctly acknowledged. The crew was informed that the aircraft was 12 miles from touchdown, and that the approach would be an SRA to Runway 23, terminating at 2 miles from touchdown. They were advised to check their minima and missed approach point. The commander responded to this transmission with a request for "co-operation with an SRE approach", to which the controller confirmed that the approach would be an SRA for Runway 23, but the termination range and the instructions to check minima and missed approach point were not repeated. The commander commented that they were not receiving the ILS. At some point after this exchange, the controller decided to continue the SRA to a termination range of 1 mile, which was the best approach available using the particular radar system in use at that time. The flight crew were not informed of this change of plan, and no information was passed to the crew regarding the latest Coventry weather, nor the latest RVR observation for Runway 23.

The Obstacle Clearance Height (OCH) for the SRA procedure to Runway 23, with a termination range of 2 miles from touchdown, is 650 feet. For an SRA termination range of 1 mile, it is 370 feet. Neither value was passed to the crew, as it was not the standard practice for ATC to do so.

A range check was passed to the aircraft at 10 miles from touchdown, and a "check wheels" was instructed. The commander responded that they were "gear down", and he requested a further range check. At this stage the aircraft was 9 miles from touchdown. The controller advised that further descent to maintain a 3° glidepath would begin at four and a half miles from touchdown.

Further headings were passed in order to intercept and follow the final approach track, and range checks were passed at each half mile interval from 6 miles. A continuous transmission was then made by the controller, as is standard practice during this type of approach. Descent instructions and advisory heights were passed from 5 miles inbound as normal. The controller had reference only to the plan position of the aircraft, and to the appropriate advisory heights for each half mile of the descent. The radar system had no facility for indicating the actual aircraft height, so the controller was not aware that the aircraft had descended below the advisory glidepath and that it had flown below the promulgated OCH.

The final centreline tracking appeared good, with only minor heading changes being required to maintain it. At 0952 hrs, while the aircraft was showing on the radar that it was inside two miles from touchdown, there was a power failure at the airport. The ATSU standby power system activated within ten seconds, reactivating the radio transmitter, but not restoring the radar system immediately. The controller called the aircraft in order to ask the crew if it was visual with the airport. There was no response. In reply to a query from the Aerodrome controller in the Visual Control Room (VCR) the RVR observer, who was close to the threshold of Runway 23, reported that he had heard the sound of a jet aircraft, followed by a loud bang. The controller then noticed a column of smoke rising above the fog bank in the final approach area and operated the crash alarm at 0954 hrs.

1.1.5   Collision and impact information

The aircraft struck a 132 kV suspension electricity transmission tower (pylon). The pylon was 86 feet high and situated on the extended centreline of Runway 23, at a distance of approximately 1.1 miles from the threshold. The elevation of the ground at this location is 291 feet amsl.

The impact with the cables and pylon triggered Alarm and Indication signals, and tripped protective circuit breakers on the power system supervisory equipment installed at the Coventry Substation. The time of the first recorded alarm signal caused by the accident was 09:52:33.72 hrs. The automatic circuit protection systems activated, which resulted in a loss of power to the airport as well as much of the surrounding area.

The impact occurred at approximately 72 feet agl with the aircraft in an almost wings level attitude. Major damage was caused to the inboard high lift devices on the left wing, and to the left engine. The consequent loss of lift on the left wing, and the thrust asymmetry, caused the aircraft to roll uncontrollably to the left. When passing through a wings vertical attitude, the left wingtip struck the gable end of a house, causing major structural damage to the property, and the wingtip to separate from the aircraft. The left roll continued until the aircraft crashed inverted into an area of woodland close to the edge of the housing conurbation. An intense fire ensued, during which a large part of the forward fuselage aft to the wheel well, including the wing centre section and the inboard portions of the wings were consumed. The five occupants suffered fatal multiple injuries on impact.

1.1.6   Witnesses

Various witnesses indicated that there was fog in the approach area at the time of the accident. They reported that the fog seemed to be generally lifting, and the visibility below the layer of low stratus cloud had improved. However, those working at the western end of an industrial estate, situated on the extended centreline just inside 2 miles from the runway threshold, indicated that visibility over the field looking towards the pylon location was very poor. The surface of the field was reported as being wet, there was a fog bank at ground level in that area, and the forward visibility was estimated to be about 50 metres.

Another observer, situated in the middle of the same industrial estate, stated that the fog in his vicinity had dispersed sufficiently that blue sky could be clearly seen directly above, but there were still banks of fog present to the northeast of the airport. Horizontal visibility at his location was hazy but not poor, and the aircraft was clearly visible passing in and out of the top of the fog bank as it passed. The aircraft's colour scheme and logos were clearly identifiable. The witness noted that the aircraft was to the south side of the normal approach track, but it was correcting from left to right as it passed. The aircraft was subsequently observed by another witness to enter a fog bank when approaching the field in which the pylon was situated.

1.2 Injuries to persons

Injuries	Crew	Passengers	Others
Fatal	3	2	-
Serious	-	-	-
Minor/None	-	-	

There were no injuries to other persons.

1.3 Damage to aircraft

The aircraft was destroyed by impact with an electricity pylon, the ground and by post-crash fire.

1.4 Other damage

The aircraft's impact with the pylon destroyed the middle pair of the three pairs of cable support arms, and the top of the pylon complete with the upper pair of arms collapsed to the ground. About 140 metres beyond the pylon, the aircraft's left wingtip struck the gable end of a terraced house causing severe structural damage. The aircraft passed over two further rows of terraced houses causing minor damage from falling debris, including damage to the ridge tiles and chimney stack of one house. The aircraft then descended inverted into Willenhall Copse destroying a lamp post at the roadside and a large number of trees by impact and fire.

1.5   Personnel information

1.5.1
Commander:	Male, aged 44 years
Licence:	Airline Transport Pilot's Licence (Algerian)
Aircraft ratings:	Boeing 737, 727, Airbus 300/310, Fokker F27
Instrument Rating:	29 October 1994
Base Check:	29 October 1994
Line Check:	2 September 1994
Medical Certificate:	30 October 1994

Flying experience:

	Total flying:	10,686 hours
	On type:	2,187 hours
	Last 90 days:	95 hours
	Last 28 days:	25 hours
	Last 24 hours:	4 hours

Previous rest period:	27 hours
Basic Training:	Company sponsored, in France Completed in 1975
Previous Operation into UK:	November 1994

No Crew Resource Management Training course had been attended.

1.5.2
First officer:	Male, aged 35 years
Licence:	Airline Transport Pilot's Licence (Algerian)
Aircraft ratings:	Boeing 737, Fokker F27, Cessna 310
Instrument Rating:	25 September 1994
Base Check:	25 September 1994
Line Check:	31 July 1994
Medical Certificate:	6 December 1994

Flying experience:

	Total flying:	2,858 hours
	On type:	2,055 hours
	Last 90 days:	76 hours
	Last 28 days:	18 hours
	Last 24 hours:	4 hours

Previous rest period:	27 hours
Basic Training:	Company sponsored, in France Completed in 1985

Previous Operation into UK: 1 December 1994

A single briefing on Crew Resource Management had been attended.

1.5.3   Air Traffic Control Officer: Female, aged 29 years
(ATCO)

Validations: Aerodrome control

Approach control

Approach radar - Plessey ACR430

Approach radar - Marconi S511

Meteorological Observer certificate

Employment at Coventry   since 29 July 1991

Duty commenced   0700 hrs on 21 December 1994

Time since last break   15 minutes

1.5.4   Air Traffic Services Assistant: Male
(ATSA)

Validations: Meteorological Observer certificate training
completed on 16 December 1994

No other validations required

Employment at Coventry   since 17 June 1992

Duty commenced   0730 hrs on 21 December 1994

Time since last break   Not relevant

1.6   Aircraft information

1.6.1   Leading particulars

Manufacturer: Boeing Commercial Airplane Company

Aircraft type: Boeing 737-2D6C

Constructor's serial number: 20758

Year of manufacture: 1973

Engines: 2 Pratt & Whitney JT8D-15 turbofan engines

No 1 Engine Serial No P695283B

No 2 Engine Serial No P688581B

Certificate of Airworthiness: Public Transport of post and cargo
validated until 17 June 1995

Certificate of Maintenance: Issued 18 December 1994
valid until 17 June 1995

Total aircraft hours (last record):   45,633 on 20 December 1994

1.6.2   Aircraft history and maintenance records

The aircraft had been operated by Air Algerie since new. It had been modified for cargo operations by the embodiment of a large cargo door at the L1 position. At the time of the accident the aircraft cabin contained a number of (empty) palletised livestock pens which engaged and locked into the rails in the cabin floor.

The operator supplied maintenance and airworthiness documentation which included Technical Log pages covering operations during the earlier part of December 1994, and worksheets covering rectifications and scheduled maintenance carried out on 18 December 1994 at Algiers. Following the impact, the cockpit area was consumed by fire, but some documents were recovered in a damaged and partially burned condition. However, these included only part of one page from the Technical Log, covering flights after the aircraft's return to the UK from Algiers. No pages had been left with any handling agents. The damaged part page concerned operations on 20 December, when 16 operating hours had been completed since the visit to Algiers, and the entries appeared to comprise the daily or pre-flight checks.

The aircraft began operations from Coventry on 5 November 1994 and continued during December, with a return to Algiers on the third of the month when some rectifications were carried out including a problem with the leading edge devices and a problem with the security of the front livestock pallet. On 15 December it was noted in the Technical log that the FDR was unserviceable. The aircraft completed 22 sectors before the recorder was replaced at Algiers on 18 December. The relevant worksheet recorded that the newly installed recorder was tested successfully[7]. It was also noted, on 15 December, that the No 3 leading edge flap had stopped in transit but cycling of the system on the ground failed to reproduce the condition. Retesting during maintenance on 18 December also failed to repeat the malfunction. The then current Certificate of Airworthiness (C of A) lapsed on 15 December, and a note drawing attention to this had been entered in the Technical Log. The corresponding action was recorded as "fait et mis à bord" (sic) ie "accomplished and put on board". No document was provided which formally extended the validity of the C of A, but on the Technical Log sheets from 16 December onwards a 20 hour extension was noted for the next scheduled maintenance which would include the C of A revalidation.

---

[7]   The FAA Master Minimum Equipment List (MMEL) allows the FDR to be inoperative provided the CVR is operating normally and repairs are carried out within three days.

On 18 December 1994 a scheduled maintenance inspection (V1, 170 hour) was carried out, and a six-monthly inspection for revalidation of the C of A. Rectification of the outstanding defects which had accrued during the operations away from Algiers was also certified. The aircraft had undergone "Block 5" of its major maintenance cycle in February 1994, and was due for a Major Overhaul at 56,515 hours and no later than 23 June 95.

1.6.3   Weight and balance

Maximum permitted Take-off Weight:	52,400 kg
Estimated Take-off Weight:	36,500 kg
Estimated Take-off Centre of Gravity (%mac):	14.5%
Maximum permitted Zero Fuel Weight:	43,100 kg
Estimated Zero Fuel Weight:	29,475 kg
Maximum permitted Landing Weight:	46,700 kg
Estimated Weight at accident:	35,500 kg
Estimated fuel on board at accident:	6,000 kg

1.6.4   Recommended approach procedures

The manufacturer's recommended approach procedures are presented in the aircraft's Operations Manual. Appendix A, Figure 1 shows the relevant extracts detailing flap extension and approach speeds. The target reference approach speed (V_{REF}) for the estimated weight in a 30° Flap configuration was 116 kt.

The Operations Manual also describes the approach technique for a non-precision approach (Appendix A, Figure 2), suggesting a descent to MDA as soon as practical after passing the final approach fix inbound, and this is shown in diagram form in Appendix A, Figure 3.

Some other operators have introduced a modified technique for the conduct of a non-precision approach for large transport aircraft, when range to touchdown information is available. Descent should be planned to follow a nominal 3° glidepath (or as specified in the particular procedure), so that the MDH/MDA[8] is reached just as the aircraft arrives at the Missed Approach Point (MAPt). On reaching the MDH/MDA, a go-around manoeuvre should then be initiated if the specified visual reference has not been established. This is intended to avoid flying any level segment at, or slightly above, the MDH while flying towards the

---

[8]   MDH is applicable to approaches conducted by reference to pressure altimeters set to QFE, and MDA to those conducted with QNH set.

MAPt and waiting for the correct visual references to appear. This may require late changes of aircraft configuration and/or power and pitch attitude changes when close to the ground. The principal, known as the "stabilised approach" technique, is now widely taught but is not detailed in the Boeing Operations Manual for 7T-VEE.

The stabilised approach technique was carried out by the crew of 7T-VEE during the previous two SRA approaches on the morning of 21 December 1994, but their technique differed significantly during the final SRA, and resulted in an unstabilised approach.

1.6.5   Flight instruments, autopilot and GPWS

1.6.5.1   Flight instruments

This aircraft was fitted with the original standard of pressure altimeters, which did not have the facility of an adjustable DH/MDH cursor. For Category 1 precision approaches, and for all non-precision approaches, the DH/MDH is referenced to the aircraft's pressure altimeters with subscales set to QFE[9], and not to the aircraft's Radio Altimeters (RAs).

The RAs on this aircraft were fitted with adjustable DH/MDH cursors. RAs read actual height above the ground directly beneath the aircraft, but are of limited value during non-precision approaches because the nature of the terrain under the approach path may not necessarily be level, flat or related to the runway threshold elevation in a meaningful way. The use of the RA height cursors for this type of approach is therefore of only secondary guidance value.

The aircraft was equipped with an aural altitude alerting system, which provided an alert tone when the aircraft was approaching the pre-set altitude. The tone was activated when the aircraft was within 1,000 feet of the pre-set value. On this aircraft, no altitude deviation alerting system was fitted.

A dual Flight Director (FD) system was fitted. A single cue command bar was located on each pilot's Attitude Director Indicator (ADI). The system was the most up to date that was available at the time of construction of the aircraft, but had fewer features than more modern FD systems. A mode selector was provided for each pilot, so that the two FDs could be operated independently. Modes available included Go-Around, Heading, VOR/LOC, Auto Approach and Manual

---

[9]   Air Algerie standard operating procedure specifies use of QFE for approaches.

Glideslope (the latter two modes for use with an ILS facility only). Also fitted was an Altitude Hold mode. When not in Altitude Hold or tracking an ILS Glideslope, the only pitch mode available was Pitch Attitude command, each mode selector having a rotary knob which the pilot could rotate to select a particular constant aircraft pitch attitude for the FD command bar. In this system, there was no facility for commanding a constant airspeed or constant rate of descent. Full pitch and roll approach guidance was therefore available from the FDs whenever the aircraft was flying an ILS approach, but the only modes available for use on a non-precision approach, such as an SRA, were Heading and Pitch Attitude. It is unlikely that the FD Pitch mode was in use at the time of the accident, because of the need to adjust continuously the pitch attitude setting during an approach whenever speed, power or configuration changes occurred and for changes in the rate of descent.

1.6.5.2   Autopilot System

The aircraft was equipped with an autopilot with pitch and roll channels. No autopilot disconnect audio warning system was fitted and therefore it was not possible to determine, from CVR evidence, whether or not the autopilot was in use (see also paragraph 1.12.2).

1.6.5.3   Ground Proximity Warning System (GPWS)

A Mark 1 GPWS was fitted, which had five warning modes available. The GPWS was not designed to detect obstacles located ahead of the aircraft's position. The five available modes were:

Mode 1   Excessive Descent Rate
Mode 2   Excessive Terrain Closure Rate
Mode 3   Altitude Loss after Take-off or Go-Around
Mode 4   Unsafe Terrain Clearance while not in the Landing Configuration
Mode 5   Below Glideslope Deviation Alert

Given the aircraft's configuration at the time of the accident no aural warnings from the GPWS were to be expected and none was heard on the CVR.

1.7   Meteorological information

1.7.1   Aftercast

An aftercast, produced from the Meteorological Office Headquarters at Bracknell, indicated that the synoptic situation at 1000 hrs showed an anticyclone of some

16

1028 mb centred over Scotland, extending a ridge of high pressure over England and Wales. The weather was very misty with fog patches, and visibility ranging between 800 metres and 1,500 metres. The mean sea level pressure was 1023 mb. The cloud was scattered or broken, base 800 to 1,000 feet amsl. The surface wind was variable at 5 kt, and the upper wind at 2,000 feet from 010°/15 kt. The mist and fog had been fairly extensive around dawn, but had largely lifted from most places by 1000 hrs.

1.7.2   Terminal Aerodrome Forecasts (TAFs)

The Terminal Aerodrome Forecast (TAF) for Coventry Airport, issued by the Birmingham Weather Centre at 0300 hrs on the AFTN system, and valid for the period 0400 to 1300 hrs was recorded as: Surface wind variable 3 kt, visibility 10 km or more, scattered cloudbase 3,000 feet, probability 30% of temporary changes between 0400 and 0900 hrs to a visibility of 800 metres in fog.

A later revision issued at 0500 hrs indicated that the temporary change in visibility would occur during the period 0600 to 0900 hrs with a visibility of 800 metres in fog and a broken cloudbase at 200 feet. The later TAF issued for the validity period 0700 to 1600 hrs showed little change in the basic data, but the temporary change had been further revised to a probability 30% of temporary changes between 0700 and 0900 hrs with a visibility of 800 metres in fog, and a broken cloudbase at 100 feet. Thus, no fog was forecast to be present after 0900 hrs in any of the TAFs.

1.7.3   Aviation Routine weather reports (METARs)

The "post-accident" observation logged at Coventry was the 0950 hrs METAR: Surface wind 020° at 6 kt, visibility 1,200 metres in mist, RVR Runway 23 1,100 metres, RVR Runway 05 greater than 1,300 metres, scattered cloudbase 700 feet, scattered cloudbase 1,200 feet, temperature 2°C, QNH 1023 mb.

Actual weather observations are taken at hourly intervals at Coventry Airport. The observations taken during the early hours of 21 December 1994, up to the time of the accident are detailed in Appendix B. No observations from Coventry were recorded in the Meteorological Office records until the 0750 hrs observation. However, the TAF valid for the period 0400 to 1300 hrs had been issued, indicating that at least some of the earlier observations had been passed by telephone to the Birmingham Meteorological Centre.

The 0400 to 1300 hrs Coventry TAF would have been available to the crew together with the pre-flight documentation in the flight briefing folder prepared by the aircraft handling agents in Amsterdam. The 0700 to 1600 hrs TAF, and the 0750 and 0850 hrs METARs for Coventry, would have been available from the Flight Briefing Unit at East Midlands Airport prior to the departure of the aircraft.

1.7.4　　　　Runway Visual Range (RVR)

The RVR measurements at Coventry are taken by the human observer method, whenever the visibility falls below 1,500 metres. The technique involves an observer, usually a member of the Airport Fire Service, taking a vehicle to each end of the Runway 05/23 in turn, adjacent to the thresholds, and noting the number of runway lights that are observed through the obscuration. These counts are transmitted to the VCR by UHF radio link. A conversion table is kept in the VCR so that the number of lights observed may be converted into an RVR value, and this is recorded on the RVR log form CA1044. The airport is not equipped with an instrumented RVR system. The RVR observations taken at Coventry Airport during the morning of 21 December 1994 are also shown in Appendix B.

The final RVR log entry was found to be in error. The recording of UHF communications between the Tower and the mobile vehicle operator tasked with RVR observations indicated that at 0940 hrs, 23 lights could be counted from the Runway 05 assessment point. From the conversion table in the Tower, this gave an RVR in excess of 1,300 metres. The vehicle was asked to take another measurement from the Runway 23 assessment point, and transited down the main runway. This RVR assessment was then carried out at 0945 hrs on Runway 23, and indicated that 20 lights were visible, converting to an RVR of 1,100 metres. This was never recorded on the RVR log (Form CA1044), but was entered correctly on the 0950 hrs METAR.

1.7.5　　　　Meteorological Observations at Coventry

The required instruments for compiling the Meteorological observations were serviceable at the time of the accident, with the exception of the cloudbase recorder, which had been unserviceable for a prolonged period.

METARs are prepared hourly, at ten minutes to each hour (H+50), by Meteorological Observer certificated ATCOs or ATSAs. These are then transmitted by teleprinter or AFTN to the Meteorological Office. For local use, the data is input into a Commodore 16 microcomputer and displayed on the Closed Circuit Television (CCTV) system in the Visual Control Room (VCR), Radar Room and Flight Briefing Unit.

Specific improvement or deterioration of any of the items in a routine report are supplied in a Special Meteorological report. They are issued between routine reports and contain only those items which are affected. The criteria for raising Special reports are specified for ATS staff in the Manual of Air Traffic Services (MATS) Part 1 (Appendix C). Special reports should be displayed immediately with the time of observation, and the compiler is required to advise the Aerodrome and Approach Controllers of the contents.

Between the routine 0850 hrs and 0950 hrs observations, the visibility at Coventry had improved above 800 metres, and the cloudbase had lifted through 200, 300 and 500 feet, all of which are specified criteria requiring a Special Observation. None was taken in this period.

1.7.6   Information from the pilot of the previous landing aircraft

The instrument rated pilot of a Piper PA-28 aircraft provided useful information regarding the actual weather conditions experienced in the approach area for the period between 0905 and 0935 hrs. During that period, the pilot was kept fully informed of the changes in the RVR by Coventry ATC. Approaches were flown using the Runway 23 ILS, the first being at 0910 hrs with an RVR of 900 metres, and the second at 0920 hrs with an RVR of 1,000 metres. On both occasions, the aircraft descended to the promulgated DH of 280 feet, and the pilot executed go-arounds because no visual references were attained. Once the weather conditions began to improve, a third attempt was made at about 0930 hrs. On that occasion, the pilot had reference to the approach lights through a gap in the fog as the aircraft reached DH and a successful landing ensued. The pilot considered that the visibility was at least one mile once below the cloudbase which was estimated to have been 200 feet. The pilot also noted that the cloud tops were at 500 to 600 feet agl, with clear blue skies and good visibility above. Gaps in the fog were perceived to be becoming larger and more widespread by the time the third approach was commenced.

1.8   Aids to navigation

1.8.1   Coventry Airport is equipped with the following instrument approach aids:

1.8.1.1   Instrument Landing System (ILS), Runway 23:

Coded 'I CT' it radiates on frequency 109.75 MHz. The Localiser is aligned with the final approach track for Runway 23, on a magnetic track of 232°M. The associated Glideslope signals, radiated on the frequency-paired channel 333.05 MHz, give a glidepath angle of 3°. This system was initially commissioned in 1990, and was fully serviceable at the time of the accident. No ILS system is available for approaches to Runway 05.

1.8.1.2   Non-Directional Beacon (NDB)

Coded 'CT' it radiates on frequency 363.5 kHz. The transmitter is located on the approach centreline of Runway 23 at a distance of 3.25 miles from the threshold. It was serviceable at the time of the accident.

1.8.1.3   Surveillance Radar Equipment (SRE)

A Marconi S511 system with colour Rickard-Miller raster scan display was serviceable and in use at the time of the accident. This equipment is approved for giving guidance for SRA approaches to 2 miles or 1 mile Radar Termination Range (RTR). It had been used for the successful SRA Approach conducted by 7T-VEE at 0340 hrs on the morning of the accident. The Coventry Radar Vectoring Area is shown in Appendix D, Figure 1. The CAA approach chart detailing the SRA procedures for Runway 23 is shown in Appendix D, Figure 2. The information is also shown in tabulated form in the AIP RAC section, Appendix D, Figure 3.

An older Plessey ACR430 system with monochrome display was serviceable at the time of the accident, but was not in use. This equipment is approved for giving guidance for SRA approaches to 1 mile or 0.5 mile RTR. This equipment was used to provide 7T-VEE with guidance during the SRA to a 0.5 mile RTR and subsequent go-around at 0735 hrs on the morning of the accident.

1.8.2   Aircraft equipment

1.8.2.1   VHF Omni-directional Radio Range (VOR)

Three VOR navigation receivers were fitted to the aircraft and were serviceable at the time of the accident. These provided the primary means of navigation for this aircraft while en route. No VOR ground stations were relevant to the approaches carried out at Coventry on the day of the accident.

1.8.2.2   Instrument Landing System (ILS)

The three VOR navigation receivers (Nos 1, 2 and AUX) were also capable of receiving ILS Localiser signals. Triple ILS Glideslope (GS) receivers were also fitted. Although there were three navigation receivers, only two, No 1 and 2, or No 1 and AUX, or No 2 and AUX, were operational and the third was in standby mode. Each pilot was provided with a Horizontal Situation Indicator (HSI). The output from the aircraft's navigation receivers was used to display the aircraft's position with respect to the pilot-selected course on the HSI, for VOR or ILS Localiser signals. ILS GS indications were also provided on the same instrument. Additionally, on each pilot's Attitude Director Indicator (ADI), a display of ILS Localiser and GS was provided. The ILS is regarded as the primary aid for making instrument approaches to airports in poor weather conditions.

The navigation receivers originally fitted to the aircraft were "Buyer Furnished Equipment" and were of a standard capable of receiving 20 ILS channels. It was the policy of the aircraft manufacturer to fit control boxes which matched the capacity of the rest of the radio equipment and so "20 channel" control boxes were fitted. The original specification for ILS Localiser installations allocated channels in the VHF band between 108.1 and 111.9 MHz, spaced at each odd decimal value, giving 20 available channels in total. As the number of ILS installations grew at adjacent airports[10], it became apparent that more than 20 channels would be required. An ICAO agreement specified that the channel spacing would be reduced, and introduced 20 extra channels spaced 50 kHz (0.05 MHz) above the existing frequencies. These frequencies became available for use by ground installations from 1976 onwards.

The original aircraft receivers were capable of being modified to meet the 40 channel standard, which was initially implemented in the USA in 1973. The control boxes required replacement before the 40 channels could be used. The Certificate of Approval of Radio Installation records that aircraft was fitted with three Collins Type 51RV 2B VOR/ILS Navigational Receivers. Only one receiver, and none of the navigational control boxes, was recovered in an

---

[10]   ILS installations have a protected range requirement to avoid interference from adjacent facilities.

identifiable condition from the wreckage. That set proved to be a type 51RV 4B, a slightly later series than that documented, and one which was capable of receiving 40 channels though these could not be used without the correct control box.

Some flight crews reported to Phoenix Aviation management that the aircraft's equipment would not operate on the Coventry ILS frequency. The Air Algerie Flight Operations management in Algiers were also informed by facsimile, but no remedial action was immediately forthcoming. In an attempt to ensure that poor weather would not disrupt the aircraft's flight programme through the winter months, Phoenix Aviation arranged for a 40 channel navigation receiver to be brought to Coventry from a UK supplier. The Air Algerie engineering staff fitted the unit, but it would not function correctly. This was consistent with the aircraft being fitted with the earlier standard of 20 channel control boxes. The replacement unit was removed and returned to the supplier, and the aircraft was restored to its former avionic condition around the beginning of December 1994.

Carriage of an ILS receiver was not mandatory under UK regulations for an aircraft making approaches to Coventry Airport.

1.8.2.3   Automatic Direction Finding (ADF)

Two ADF receivers were installed, each receiver driving one pointer on each pilot's Radio Magnetic Indicator (RMI). The units were tuned to the Coventry NDB frequency 363.5 kHz at the time of the accident.

1.8.2.4   Distance Measuring Equipment (DME)

A DME receiver was fitted, with a distance measurement display located in a corner of each pilot's HSI. There were no DME stations relevant to the SRA approaches carried out at Coventry, and there were no adjacent stations that would have provided useful distance information to the crew.

1.9   Communications

A complete series of recordings and transcripts were studied in order to follow the progress of the flight within UK airspace and during each of the approaches made during the duty period of the accident crew.

The radio callsign used by the crew for the sector from Amsterdam and diversion to East Midlands was "Fastcargo 702". The final sector to Coventry used the callsign "Fastcargo 702P", the "P" suffix indicating a positioning flight for ATC flight plan purposes.

Additionally, at Coventry Airport, UHF radiotelephony transmissions between the VCR and airport surface vehicles was recorded. This included the vehicle used while taking RVR observations.

1.10   Aerodrome information

1.10.1   Physical characteristics

Coventry Airport has two hard surfaced runways:

17/35   Asphalt, 815 metres long, 30 metres wide.
05/23   Asphalt, 1615 metres long (*), 46 metres wide.
(*) includes 210 metre starter extension, block paved, which is not available to aircraft with underslung engines (such as the Boeing 737).

Instrument Approach procedures are available for Runway 05/23 only. Approach, threshold and runway lighting is therefore provided for this runway. Runway 23 is equipped with 416 metres of high intensity coded centreline approach lights with two crossbars, high intensity green threshold lights with elevated high intensity green wing bars, elevated high intensity white bi-directional runway lights with a low intensity omni-directional white component, red end lights plus red edge lighting to the 93 metre grass stopway. A Precision Approach Path Indicator (PAPI) system, set at 3°, is situated on the left side of Runway 23, 365 metres in from the threshold (the normal touchdown aiming point), with a Minimum Eye Height over Threshold (MEHT) of 56 feet.

1.10.2   Air Traffic Services Unit (ATSU)

The Coventry ATSU and Visual Control Room (VCR) is located at the western end of the airport, atop the operations building. Its facilities are somewhat dated. The Approach Radar room was co-located in one corner of the VCR and screened by boarded partitioning. There was an open entrance to the radar room, which did not eliminate background noise intrusion from the VCR.

There was a CCTV display of the latest weather observation and a four digit repeater display of RVR in front of the Aerodrome Controller in the VCR, and in the radar room, although these were not situated atop the display console for the Marconi S511 Radar. The digital RVR display did not indicate to which runway the measurement applied.

The complement of ATS staff in on duty at the time of the accident comprised one ATCO acting as Aerodrome controller and one ATCO operating as Approach/Approach Radar controller.

Also on duty in the VCR from 0730 hrs was an ATSA. During the week prior to the accident, he had successfully completed his Meteorological Observer certificate training course. This was the second time that he had been on duty since the completion of the course, and he was allocated responsibility for compiling the Meteorological observations, and the calculation and recording of RVR observations, along with his routine duties, for the period prior to the accident.

Guidance on the training of ATS personnel in the preparation of aerodrome weather reports was published by the CAA in an Aeronautical Information Circular, number 62/1994. Relevant extracts from this circular are presented in Appendix E.

1.11 Flight recorders

1.11.1 Flight Data Recorder (FDR)

1.11.1.1 FDR fitted to the aircraft

The type fitted was a SFIM (Société Française d'Instruments de Mesure) A2615 photographic recorder. It was located in the cabin roof at the rear of the aircraft. The recording medium was recovered undamaged after the accident.

This type of FDR uses a light sensitive paper strip which is contained in a removable light-proof cassette. The FDR installed in 7T-VEE had been changed in Algiers on 18 December 1994, prior to the accident . When the paper was removed from the cassette and developed at the Centre d'Essais en Vol at Brétigny, it was found that the FDR had been working only intermittently. A takeoff and climb of approximately 19 minutes was recorded from Algiers, followed by a break in the recording before a landing from which there was a normal shutdown. Another takeoff and climb lasting 17 minutes followed. Examination of the runway heading indicated that this was probably a flight from Coventry, and this was the last recorded data. The accident flight was not recorded, and it was not possible to determine when, in the period since the change of cassette, the recorder had stopped working.

1.11.1.2   International Standards for Flight Data Recorders

In recent years, the use of engraving metal foil recorders has been prohibited by some states. In March 1995, the ICAO Flight Recorder Panel recommended that Annex 6 to the Convention on International Civil Aviation should be amended to include a Recommended Practice that the use of photographic film recorders be discontinued by 1996.

Annex 6 sets the standard for the parameters to be recorded by the FDR as those that should have been present in this case. There is also a recommendation that, for aircraft types such as the Boeing 737, additional parameters indicating aircraft attitude, flight control positions and engine power should be recorded.

1.11.2   Cockpit Voice Recorder (CVR)

The aircraft was equipped with a Fairchild model A100 CVR, which was mounted at the rear of the aft baggage hold. The recorder was recovered from the aircraft on site, it was undamaged apart from external sooting due to the post-impact fire. A satisfactory replay was obtained using AAIB replay equipment.

The CVR covered a 30 minute period which included the whole of the final flight from East Midlands. The four tracks contained a pilot's, co-pilot's and flight engineers Radio Telephony (RT) transmissions, and an area microphone. Crew conversation was recorded on the area microphone, as well as the RT transmissions relayed through the cockpit speakers, and any other noises. This made it difficult to pick up crew conversation during RT transmissions, and particularly during the final SRA when the RT transmissions by ATC were continuous.

A transcript was produced for the flight from East Midlands, with the assistance of an Air Algerie pilot to translate parts of the crew conversation from French and Arabic. Extracts from the transcript are at Appendix F. The recording stopped when the aircraft hit the pylon, due to the interruption of the aircraft power supply to the CVR.

1.11.2.1   CVR Audio Data

An analysis of the sounds on the area microphone was made in order to determine the engine power levels during the flight. These figures are included in the extracts in Appendix F. There was no evidence of any engine failure, and the power levels appeared normal. However, due to the high audio level and continuous nature of the radiotelephony transmissions from ATC, it was not possible to determine engine power levels during the final descent phase of the approach.

1.12   **Wreckage and impact information**

1.12.1   Accident site

The site was on the extended centreline of Runway 23 at Coventry Airport and extended inbound for 260 metres from the 132 kV electricity pylon with which the aircraft had collided. The pylon was 1.1 miles from the threshold of Runway 23, and 1.27 miles from the nominal touchdown point. The elevation of the pylon base was 291 feet amsl.

The trajectory of the aircraft following its collision with the pylon, which was situated in an open field, took it over the corner of a housing estate before its impact with the ground in Willenhall Copse. In the field immediately down track of the pylon, items of wreckage were found which comprised most of the left wing's No 2 and No 3 slats, other fragmented leading edge and cowl material, the outboard aft flap and the left engine pylon fairing. Both nose leg doors were also found here. Some 140 metres from the pylon, a 5 feet span length of the aircraft's left wingtip was found lodged in a tree next to a house. The house had impact damage forming a clear imprint of the wingtip on its gable end wall. The wingtip under-surface and the adjacent wing under-surface found with the aircraft in the final impact area both had heavy scoring damage matching the contact with the wall. When the wing hit the house the aircraft had been rolling to the left with the wings passing through the vertical. Some other debris from the left wing's collision with the wall and fragments of pylon which had been carried with the aircraft were found amongst the houses and had caused damage to them.

The aircraft descended almost fully inverted to crash just beyond the houses into Willenhall Copse. Initial impact was on the cockpit roof and the disintegrated cockpit and front fuselage were carried forward by the rest of the fuselage and the wing centre section. The wings were broken up by collisions with mature trees within the copse and the engines separated from their support pylons. The forward fuselage and wings were then enveloped by fire which caused very severe damage to the remains of the cockpit.

Appendix G gives a detailed description and analysis of the pylon impact.

1.12.2   Flight Deck information

The subscale settings of the commander's and first officer's altimeters were both found to be 1013 mb (29.92 in Hg). This was the notified QFE for Coventry Airport Runway 23 at the time of the accident. The digital height indication (mechanical drum type) on the commander's altimeter was trapped with the left three drums at zero and the right end, "tens of feet" drum at an indication of 60 feet. The digital display on the first officer's altimeter gave an indication close to zero with the right end drum ("hundreds of feet") slightly displaced from zero towards "1".

The MDH cursor on the commander's RA was found to be set at zero, and the first officer's was set at 200 feet. The design was such that when the radio height reached the cursor setting on each instrument during an approach, then an MDH warning light would illuminate on that corresponding pilot's instrument panel.

Little reliable evidence was obtained from the Flight Director control panels. The commander's mode selector was at "AUTO/APP" and the first officer's at "VOR/LOC" but in both cases there was damage which suggested that the knob may have been rotated in the crash. The commander's Pitch command control was at "10° up" and the first officer's at zero, with no evidence in either case that the knob might have been rotated in the impact. On the Autopilot control panel the mode selector was found at "MAN" and the Pitch mode selector at "OFF".

1.12.3   Systems examination

The positions of the various primary and secondary flying controls were examined on site. The extensive impact and fire damage in the cockpit area precluded meaningful inspection of the flight deck controls. In an attempt to establish their settings, measurements of actuator extensions were taken. These were compared with graphical data supplied by the manufacturer to obtain as much pre-impact position data as possible. The extension of the screw-jack rods of the trailing edge flap indicated that they were at approximately 30°. The majority of the hydraulic actuators for the leading edge slats showed these to be fully extended, although some had obviously moved on impact. It was not possible to determine the pre-impact positions of the aileron or elevator controls, because of the mechanical reversion features of the actuators. The rudder actuators, whilst not possessing the same manual reversion capability, were still free to float to an arbitrary position.

The rudder and stabiliser trim actuators were measured to establish their pre-impact settings. The former was found to indicate approximately 12° left rudder trim, and the latter approximately 8 units of stabiliser trim. However, both can be mechanically cable-operated and were therefore subject to the effects of dissimilar cable pulling during the impact sequence. This appeared to have occurred in the case of the rudder trim actuator.

No evidence was found of any pre-impact anomalies with the primary or secondary flying controls, although a detailed inspection of the complete control circuits was impossible due to the severe impact damage and post-crash fire in the centre/forward fuselage area. Examination of the aircraft's final flight profile tended to confirm the absence of any uncommanded inputs to the flying controls.

1.12.4   Powerplants examination

Both engines had separated from their wing mountings but were found in the main wreckage area in close proximity to their respective wing attachments. The thrust reversers of both engines had detached, but were found to be in the stowed (forward thrust) position with the locks engaged.

The Inlet Guide Vane (IGV) and front accessory drive group assemblies of both engines had been torn away. The outer casing had fragmented and separated from the IGV assembly of the No 1 engine but most of the vanes were still attached to the bearing housing. These vanes had severe impact damage which had cut them and distorted them and which had clearly been caused by pylon material (girder and possibly cable). This damage was sufficient to have caused problems with the stable operation of the engine, in addition to problems arising from the ingestion of pylon and intake fragments. The No 2 engine assembly and its inlet guide vanes were extensively fragmented from ground impact.

Damage to both engine fan assemblies was extensive with all blades showing damage to both leading and trailing edges from foreign object ingestion. More than half of the fan blades in Engine No 1 had broken off at the roots in rearward (counter-rotational) bending and the remaining blades were bent in that direction. The second stage IGVs were intact but damaged and the second stage fan blades showed little bending damage but had suffered impacts on their leading and trailing edges. In engine No 2 all the first stage fan blades had been stripped in rearward bending. The second stage IGVs had been destroyed and the second stage fan blades were all bent rearwards. The damage to the fans appeared consistent with ingestion of foreign objects or impact with the ground at a relatively low power setting, the rotational damage being more severe on engine No 2 than on No 1.

There was no evidence of an uncontained failure and no metal spatter was observed in either exhaust case or jet pipe. Carbon deposits in the turbine exhausts of both engines appeared normal in colour and distribution.

The rotational damage on each engine was sufficient to show that it had been operating at a speed above idle but not at high power. Engine No 1 had suffered two distinct impacts. The first was with the electricity pylon, which had destroyed the intake cowling and damaged the inlet guide vanes. Following this collision, it is probable that the engine surged and had lost some power by the time the aircraft hit the ground. Engine No 2 was not so directly affected by the collision and gave evidence of being at higher power on ground impact.

1.12.5   Fuel samples

Fuel samples were obtained from both engines. The sample from the No 2 engine was obtained entirely from the engine fuel filter, but on the No 1 engine the fuel system was disrupted and had partially drained, consequently the sample was obtained from a variety of engine sources. The samples were analysed by the Fuels and Lubricants Department, DRA Woolwich. It was concluded that they complied with the specification requirements apart from a small amount of sediment in each sample, which was not considered significant.

1.13   Medical and pathological information

Post-mortem information did not reveal any significant medical conditions in the flight crew which may have contributed to the accident. Identification of the bodies was made difficult by the extensive fire which had ensued, and ante-mortem records were not available for the flight deck crew.

1.14   Fire

Witnesses reaching the wreckage site at an early stage indicated that the fire started and spread progressively a short time after the initial impact with the ground. The initial multiple small fires grew into an intense fire which affected and partially consumed the forward fuselage and the badly damaged inboard sections of both wings. No evidence was found to show that any fire had developed whilst the aircraft was still in flight following its collision with the pylon.

The local authority Fire Service, alerted by witnesses to the accident, attended the scene within 10 minutes. The Airport Fire Service vehicles also attended, but had some initial difficulty in locating the wreckage due to the poor visibility and the indirect nature of the road access from the airport to the site.

1.15 Survival aspects

Two seats were fitted at the rear of the cabin for the use of the stock handlers travelling with the aircraft. The engineer normally occupied one of the two observer's seats in the flight deck. There were no flight attendants on board, so the stock handlers were normally the only cabin occupants during the return journeys to Coventry. A witness at East Midlands indicated that there were two cushions present on the floor of the forward part of the cabin during the turnround. It was in this area that the bodies of the two stockhandlers were located after the accident; there was no evidence to suggest that they had used the seats and harnesses available for them. The nature of the final impact was such that the floor attachments for these rear seats remained intact. Fire did not destroy the rear of the aircraft, although there was some smoke damage. It is possible that the impact would have been survivable for any occupants of the two rear seats with properly fastened seat belts.

Witnesses arriving first at the scene of the accident reported that initially they were able to enter the rear and centre cabin of the aircraft but were not able to locate any survivors. The fire intensified, and the witnesses were forced to retreat away from the wreckage. All commented on the strong smell of fuel that was present at that time.

The flight deck and forward fuselage was completely destroyed during the initial ground impact and subsequent fire. It was assessed that there was no possibility of survival for the occupants of the flight deck or forward cabin.

1.16 Tests and research

1.16.1 Confirmation of area radar data

Recorded secondary radar data was obtained from the Clee Hill area radar head; position 52° 24'N 002°36'W, elevation 1,760 feet amsl. Using an AAIB computer program, data was converted to Ordnance Survey grid co-ordinates and plotted on 1:50,000 scale for chart overlay.

Radar data is stored on magnetic tapes, which are normally preserved for a period of 30 days before being re-used. About one month of data was therefore available for this investigation. Information on the recorded visibility was extracted from the Coventry ATSU Meteorological log book for the arrival times of 7T-VEE over the previous month. It was apparent that the aircraft had landed after SRAs on a number of occasions within that period, when the recorded visibility was below 8 km (5 miles). The relevant secondary radar data was extracted and covered ten SRAs made by 7T-VEE prior to the day of the accident, and the three made during the morning of 21 December 1994.

Additionally, in order to confirm the accuracy of the plotted radar data, investigators conducted a trial using a Cessna Citation II on 24 January 1995. This aircraft was flown, using a pre-arranged unique radar transponder squawk, on an autopilot coupled ILS to Runway 23 at Coventry, and then on three SRA approaches using the Marconi S511 radar. The trial was conducted in good weather conditions and centreline tracking was confirmed both electronically and visually. The radar data was subsequently analysed using the same methods as for the accident data. It was concluded that there were no problems with the centreline tracking available from the Marconi S511 radar system in use at the time of the accident, and that the recorded area radar data was sufficiently accurate.

Further analysis was carried out using the height information recorded during the approaches made by 7T-VEE , details of which are presented in Section 2.

1.16.2   Checks for erroneous ILS indications

An additional task conducted during the radar flight trial was to check for any misleading indications on the ILS display. With the navigation receivers set to frequencies of 109.7 and 109.8 MHz in turn (ie immediately adjacent to the ILS frequency 109.75 MHz), no spurious or erroneous indications on the ILS displays were noted, and the relevant 'OFF' flag indications were obtained correctly.

1.16.3   Assessment of possible visual cues

Since it was considered possible that the crew may have mistakenly identified other ground features along the approach path as the approach lights or runway threshold, investigators also flew a light helicopter on a number of visual approaches to Runway 23 from a 4 miles final distance in good visibility. Photographs were taken at intervals along the track while following a normal 3° glidepath and from a lower glidepath angle. Two of the photographs are presented in Appendix H, showing the aspect of the approach area from about 2 miles out.

1.17   Organisational and management information

1.17.1   Parties involved with the operation

Phoenix Aviation was a British owned and registered private limited company, founded in 1981. Its Managing Director had considerable farming and flying experience, held a current Airline Transport Pilot's Licence, and was type rated on

Boeing 707 aircraft. The company's primary business was the arrangement of charter operations for various cargo and passenger aircraft, mostly Boeing 707's of African carriers. It did not hold an Air Operator's Certificate (AOC), but relied on those airlines that it contracted to hold the required AOC. The company went into receivership in July 1995.

Race Cargo Airlines is a Ghanaian company, registered in Accra, Ghana. It holds a Ghanaian AOC, initially validated for the operation of Boeing 707 aircraft. The company had done business with Phoenix Aviation prior to the start of this operation.

Air Algerie is the state airline carrier of Algeria, based in Algiers. It operates a large fleet of some 47 aircraft, including Boeing 727, Boeing 737, Boeing 767, Airbus 310, Fokker F27 and Lockheed L-100 types. The Boeing 737 fleet numbered 16 aircraft of which three, including the accident aircraft, were equipped with a large forward cargo door.

The Department of Transport (DOT), International Aviation (IA) Directorate, holds the responsibility for the issue of permits to operate non scheduled flights for commercial purposes from and to UK airport

1.17.2   Background to the operation

Phoenix Aviation had been approached by a livestock trading company during August 1994, in order to ascertain the economic viability of the transport of live calves by air to the continent. There was, at that time, a widening embargo on this type of traffic by marine ferry companies, which was induced by public opinion and protest against the practice of live animal exports.

With regard to the specifications laid down in the Live Animals Regulations by the International Air Transport Association (IATA), various aircraft types were evaluated for the operation. The optimum aircraft for this operation was assessed to be the Boeing 737-200 series. Through an air charter broker, Air Algerie offered the lease of one Boeing 737 cargo aircraft. The airline had previous operational experience of the carriage of livestock by air. Many of its pilots had undergone their initial flying training in the UK. The company had a good degree of experience in European operations by virtue of its scheduled passenger and freight services.

1.17.3   Leasing contract

The lease for the aircraft was negotiated on the basis that Air Algerie provided the Aircraft, Crew, Maintenance and Insurance cover (an ACMI lease), and the contract was effective from 20 October 1994 initially between Air Algerie and Phoenix Aviation. The operation of the aircraft was paid for on a cost per flying hour basis, with an agreed guaranteed minimum utilisation. The charterer was required to fund the costs of fuel, en route navigation charges, landing charges, ground handling, taxes, positioning flights, crew ground transportation, hotel accommodation and crew allowances.

The contract stipulated that the charterer should obtain all the necessary takeoff, landing and overflight authorisations. The aircraft was to retain its registration and owner's colour scheme, but another stipulation was that the flights made within the scope of the agreement should operate under the flight number held by the charterer. This would ensure that any en route navigation charges would be invoiced to the charterer directly.

In order to achieve this, an operator holding an Air Operator's Certificate and an ICAO allocation of flight number designator and radio callsign was required to participate. Because of its previous dealings with Race Cargo Airlines of Ghana, Phoenix Aviation agreed with that company the use of its name, flight designator ("ACE") and radio callsign ("FASTCARGO"). Race Cargo Airlines had no other involvement in the export operation, nor in the actual operation of the aircraft.

The contract specified that Air Algerie's crews would observe the specific flight instructions relating in particular to the frequency of the flights that was given by the charterer. It also specified that, for essential safety reasons, the aircraft crew may postpone or cancel the operations in view of atmospheric or technical conditions, or reduce the authorised carrying capacity if so required by unfavourable weather conditions or operating constraints.

There was therefore no doubt that the ultimate responsibility for the technical operation of the aircraft was retained by Air Algerie, and that all flight operations were to be conducted in accordance with the company's operations manuals and limitations.

1.17.4   Operation of the aircraft

7T-VEE arrived in the United Kingdom on 20 October 1994. Initial operations commenced out of Bournemouth International Airport later the same day. The primary destination for these flights was Amsterdam. A full listing of the aircraft's operations during the period leading up to the accident is shown in Appendix J.

Some local opposition to the nature of these flights was encountered during the first two weeks of operation, and it was decided by Phoenix Aviation to switch the base of operations to Coventry Airport which was, in any event, closer to that company's headquarters. After some objections, and successful legal action by Phoenix Aviation, operations from there became almost routine.

Air Algerie crews were located in hotel accommodation close to Coventry Airport, and operated the single aircraft on a series of flights to either Amsterdam, Rennes or Nantes (France). Crews would spend one or two weeks in the UK before returning home. Replacement crews would then take over the operation. Flights were scheduled to operate in a four hour repetitive cycle, each departing from Coventry with 191 calves contained in six palletised pens. The return flights would arrive with empty pallets, ready for subsequent reloading. Departures were scheduled at 0830, 1230, 1630 hrs etc. throughout the day and night, in order to achieve the required total of over 5,000 calves per week. The 2030 hrs planned departure flight was left unused for contingency purposes each day.

The loading of each of the transport flights was carried out under the supervision of the Veterinary Service of the UK Ministry of Agriculture Fisheries and Food, who were responsible for ensuring animal welfare during transportation, and approved the optimum stock packing density for the animals. There was a requirement for two stock handlers to fly with the aircraft to ensure animal welfare. The stock handlers were employed by Phoenix Aviation for the task. Two seats with lap harnesses were fitted in the rear fuselage for their use, to the rear of the stock pens.

In response to public protests and demonstrations about the nature of the flights, there was a considerable Police presence at the airport when the flights were preparing to depart. It had been agreed with the Police that weekend operations would be scaled down in order to release officers for other duties. This meant that for two days each week, from Saturday afternoon until midday on Monday, fewer sectors were operated and the opportunity was sometimes taken by Air Algerie to return the aircraft to Algiers for maintenance.

Two Air Algerie ground engineers were located at Coventry to carry out routine checks during the aircraft turn-rounds. Each in turn would fly with the aircraft in order to carry out refuelling, turn-round inspections, and rectification of minor defects that may have arisen. The ground engineers were not allowed to travel to Algeria each week because of visa restrictions. Any defects with the aircraft were noted as "carried forward" items in the technical log, and rectification action was taken by company engineers whenever the aircraft returned to Algiers. The aircraft would then return to Coventry with a replacement flight deck crew, and with the defects rectified, at the end of each weekend.

The 0830 hrs programme slot on Monday mornings was not used for a flight, but was reserved for a crew briefing period at the hotel. During this time, a representative of Phoenix Aviation would brief the crew on the week's flying programme and destinations, and pay the crew allowances. One senior pilot at the hotel would be nominated as temporary base liaison Captain for the week, and the crew allocations would be mutually decided. The final programme, with crew allocations, was then forwarded to Air Algerie headquarters by facsimile. Arrangements for crew transport from and to the hotel were made by Phoenix Aviation representatives. Each crew would often operate four flight sectors which resulted in a normal duty period of around 10 hours duration.

1.17.5   Air Algerie Flight Time Limitations (FTL) scheme

The normal pre-flight crew report time at the airport was 75 minutes prior to the scheduled departure time. The Air Algerie FTL scheme restricted planned night duties to a normal maximum of four sectors, and to a maximum duty duration of 7 hours 45 minutes, for night operations falling within the hours of 2100 to 0500 hrs. Crews were also normally restricted to a maximum of six hours actual flight time within that specified duty period, reducing to 5 hours 30 minutes when a fifth sector was operated. A note indicated that the scheme allowed the operation of a fifth sector under exceptional circumstances, for use in case of emergency repairs, unforeseen imperative operational reasons, and for safety reasons. There was, however, no limitation quoted for the maximum extra commander's discretionary duty time allowable in the event of having to operate a fifth sector.

The pilots at Coventry appeared to have agreed locally that, because of the regular nature of the routes, the short flight times, and the ready provision of Meteorological and NOTAM information by the duty Phoenix Aviation representative, the crews would be able to reduce the pre-flight report period to 45 minutes in an attempt to remain within the normal duty period limitations. Had the aircraft arrived back at Coventry by 0730 hrs as planned, then the normal FTL limitations would have been observed. However, because of the diversion and subsequent positioning flight, the crew had been on duty for just over ten hours at the time of the accident, an exceedence of some 2 hours 10 minutes above that permitted normally.

Under UK FTL schemes, when operating four (or more) sectors, a crew starting duty after 2200 hrs local time, is allowed a maximum night duty period of nine hours, with an additional absolute maximum of three hours of commander's discretionary time for use when unforeseen circumstances occur, such as a weather diversion.

1.17.6   Flight Safety Management

Many airlines now have Flight Safety Management (FSM) functions within their Operations Departments. The purpose of FSM organisations is to provide a company wide focus on operational safety matters in conjunction with other departments. Liaison with other airlines' flight safety organisations is also important in order to discuss common operational issues, often involving dialogue with the aircraft manufacturers and airworthiness authorities. FSM organisations are also tasked with identifying new developments within the industry, and providing a basis for their introduction into the company. They are also responsible for airport and aircraft security issues, and for environmental issues where appropriate. A good FSM organisation will also provide some form of newsletter to flight crews, highlighting specific flight safety issues, and thus acting as a general safety refresher which is additional to that carried out during the routine six-monthly recurrent flight training programmes. A "feedback" reporting service, which may be confidential, can also be provided to enable flight crews to report and comment on significant operational factors that may affect flight safety. It also provides a more direct channel to operational management than routine paperwork would allow. Independent advice can be given by the FSM organisation to the airline management on the preventative action needed to eliminate or avoid reported hazards and anomalies.

At the time of the accident, Air Algerie had no FSM organisation.

1.17.7   Crew Resource Management

Crew Resource Management (CRM)[11] is a development from the initial Human Factors training now given to flight crews. CRM training is a comprehensive scheme for improving crew performance which addresses the entire crew

---

[11]   For a fuller description refer to ICAO Circular 217-AN/132 Chapter 2.

population. It can extend to all forms of crew training, and concentrates on crew member's attitudes and behaviour, and their impact on flight safety. It provides an opportunity for individuals to examine their behaviour and make individual decisions on how to improve teamwork, within the aircraft and with outside agencies. The crew should come to be regarded as a trained single unit, when operating the aircraft.

In Air Algerie, until this accident occurred, the only CRM training that was carried out was for newly appointed First Officers. They were given a short briefing on the concepts of CRM. Current Captains were not given any CRM courses.

1.17.8   Official monitoring of AOC standards

The Algerian Department of Civil Aviation had delegated the inspection of flight operations to Air Algerie. Selected senior training Captains from the airline were tasked with carrying out a monitoring function, on behalf of the Department, in addition to their normal duties and routine proficiency checks.

1.18   Additional information

1.18.1   Airport development, housing and pylon construction

The airport became operational at its present site in 1936, then being a wholly grass landing area. Construction of the hard surfaced main 05/23 Runway was commenced in 1959, and it became operational in 1961. The starter extension at the 23 threshold was block paved in 1989, but the landing threshold itself for this runway was not moved.

Some seven years before this accident, the airport was selected as the hub for an extensive night parcel delivery operation, and night freighter activity has developed extensively since then. At the time of the accident, the airport was operational on a 24 hour basis, except at weekends. It has become the sixth busiest airport in the UK in terms of freight flown. The total number of aircraft movements (takeoffs and landings) recorded during 1994 was in excess of 56,600, ranking the airport as number 21 in the UK. Over 6,900 of these movements were classified as Air Transport Movements, ranking the airport as number 33 in this category.

At the time of the accident, the airport was owned and operated by Coventry City Council, but was the subject of a joint venture proposal between the City Council and a private company. It was managed primarily by an Airport Manager. In his absence, responsibility for operation of the Airport passed, in order of seniority, to the Manager Air Traffic Services (ATS), the Deputy Manager ATS, or the duty ATC Watch Manager.

The housing estate adjacent to the accident site in Willenhall was constructed during 1957. No planning consultation with the CAA was necessary at that time, and none took place. Under current requirements for consultation with the CAA, the area falls within the 15.2 metre height protection area, but traditional two storey residential developments would not necessitate consultation before the grant of planning permission.

The electricity pylon was constructed in 1951, and was 86 feet agl (377 feet amsl). Its position was 1.1 miles from the Runway 23 threshold, and on the extended centreline. It did not encroach into the 1:50 approach plane, and thus was not considered as an approach obstacle. However, the adjacent pylon to the south of the extended centreline was slightly taller and was the dominant obstacle in the determination of the relevant approach minima.

1.18.2   Public Safety Zones

Public Safety Zones (PSZs) are described in Appendix K, and details of UK airports which have PSZs are shown in Appendix L. No PSZs have been placed at Coventry Airport because of the amount of air traffic using the airport. In 1994, there were an average of 4,717 per movements per month, of which 575 were classified as air transport movements. These figures fall significantly short of the figures quoted for the implementation of PSZs. The location of the accident site in this case was, in any event, outside of the area that would have been protected by a PSZ of either current dimension.

The DOT is currently undertaking a review of the policy on PSZs. CAA sourced statistics show that in the UK, over a ten year period to the end of 1992, there were only 5 accidents to transport aircraft with an Maximum allowable Take-Off Weight (MTOW) > 5,700 kg which occurred during the takeoff/initial climb and approach/landing phases of flight. The total number of recorded movements during this period in the UK was in excess of 15 million, giving an observed accident rate of 0.33 per million movements.

The current review will use further analysis of relevant international accident statistical data, and risk contour modelling. It will consider whether any changes are required to the existing size and shape of PSZs. It will also consider whether simple rules related to traffic levels and to types of traffic can be drawn up on the setting of PSZs at airports.

1.18.3   UK Aeronautical Information Publication (AIP)

The document providing the necessary details for aircraft operations within the UK is the AIP, published as CAP 32. This document is published in accordance with the provisions of Annex 15 to the Convention on International Civil Aviation. It provides information on aeronautical facilities, regulations and ground organisation for the safe conduct of civil aviation in the UK. Its primary object is to meet the needs of those engaged in flying operations, but consideration has also been given to its use for the planning of operations and as a guide to civil aviation generally in this country. Additionally, it is the official document used for notifying the requirements of the Air Navigation Order (ANO).

CAP 32 contains sections dealing with Air Traffic Rules and Services (RAC), Aerodromes (AGA), Communications (COM), Meteorology (MET), Facilitation (FAL), Search and Rescue (SAR) and Aeronautical Charts (MAP).

1.18.4   Permits to operate flights

Article 88 of the UK Air Navigation Order 1989 (as amended), requires permission from the Secretary of State for Transport before an aircraft registered outside the UK (or any State of the European Union) can be used for cargo operations from an airport within the UK. The details regarding permit applications are described in the FAL section of the AIP.

Details of this requirement, and the permit application system are given in Appendix M. This procedure is consistent with the obligations of Article 33 of the Convention on International Civil Aviation (Chicago, 1944) which states:

'Recognition of certificates and licenses

Certificates of airworthiness and certificates of competency and licenses issued or rendered valid by the contracting State in which the aircraft is registered, shall be recognised as valid by the other contracting States, provided that the requirements under which such certificates or licenses were issued or rendered valid are equal to or above the minimum standards which may be established from time to time pursuant to this Convention.'

In this case, prior permission was required from the Department of Transport, International Aviation Directorate (DOT/IA) for the operation of the series of cargo flights using the Air Algerie aircraft. The leasing contract stated that the application was the responsibility of the charterer.

For commercial reasons, it was decided by Phoenix Aviation to use the flight number designator and radio callsign of Race Cargo Airlines of Ghana. The necessary permissions were therefore requested detailing Race Cargo Airlines, rather than Phoenix Aviation, as the aircraft operator.

The DOT/IA sought to confirm that Race Cargo Airlines, rather than Air Algerie, held an AOC to cover the export flights. To facilitate this, Race Cargo Airlines was requested by Phoenix Aviation to add 7T-VEE to its AOC. Additionally, updated insurance documentation was required from Air Algerie's insurers, indicating that both Phoenix Aviation and Race Cargo Airlines were included in the cover on the insurance certificate for the aircraft. These arrangements took some time to organise and complete. Meanwhile the flight operations, which had begun at Bournemouth, continued. In facsimile letters to Phoenix Aviation, the DOT/IA drew their attention to the illegality of operating without the issue of an Article 88 Permit by the Department before each flight.

Application for the necessary permits had been submitted for flights up to the end of November, but delays in the provision of the required documentation from sources in Algeria and Ghana meant that they had not been issued. No applications were submitted for the flights which took place in December.

1.18.5   Instrument approach procedures and obstacle clearance criteria

Details of instrument approach procedures to airports within the UK are published by the CAA both by diagram (Appendix D, Figure 2), and in tabular form (Appendix D, Figure 3) in the AIP. Both presentations give details of the appropriate Obstacle Clearance Height (OCH) for each of four aircraft categories A, B, C, D.

These aircraft categories are established on the basis of the nominal threshold speed for the maximum permitted landing weight of the aircraft type, the slowest (lightest) aircraft being in category A. The Boeing 737 series is categorised as C for approach minima purposes, having a nominal threshold speed in the band between 121 and 140 kt IAS.

The OCH is calculated to take account of the minimum specified clearance above the height of the dominant (highest) obstacle in the final approach area. This minimum clearance varies for each type of approach aid. Aircraft category and OCH are used as a basis for the determination of the DH/MDH to which an aircraft may descend during an instrument approach procedure, without the crew having visual reference to the landing runway or approach lighting. In the case of an SRA, the OCH does not vary with speed category, as it is based on the assumption that the aircraft is flying level, rather than descending, at the Missed Approach Point (MAPt). If an aircraft were to sink below the OCH, for example during the initiation of a go-around manoeuvre, then the minimum specified clearance from the dominant obstacle would not be assured. A nominal 50 feet has been allowed in the OCH assessment to account for any altimeter error.

For an SRA, the minimum clearance from the OCH to the top of the highest obstacle within the final approach primary area is 75 metres (246 feet). It is defined in ICAO Document 8168, Procedures for Air Navigation Services, Aircraft Operations, Volume II, Construction of Visual and Instrument Flight Procedures. It is also reiterated in the UK AIP, RAC section.

The primary area considered for obstacle clearance begins at the Final Approach Fix (FAF), which is at 5 miles radar range in the case of procedures to Runway 23 at Coventry, and ends at the MAPt, which is the appropriate Radar Termination Range (RTR). The width of the primary area increases with the distance away from the radar antenna.

In the specific case of Runway 23 at Coventry, the dominant obstacle controlling the OCH for the 1 mile and 0.5 mile RTR approaches was an electricity pylon adjacent to that involved in this accident, which was positioned to the south side of the runway extended centreline. That pylon was depicted on the Aerodrome Obstacle Chart, Type A, as being 384 feet amsl (or 119 feet above the threshold elevation of Runway 23). The OCH was thus calculated by adding 246 feet minimum clearance to the 119 feet obstacle height, with a result of 365 feet. This was then rounded up to the nearest 10 feet, giving the published OCH 370 feet.

In the case of the 2 miles RTR, the promulgated OCH is 650 feet because of further obstacle clearance considerations. Additionally, because of the difference between the Aerodrome Reference Point elevation (281 feet amsl) and the Runway 23 threshold elevation (265 feet amsl), all of the minima calculations and radar advisory heights are based on the touchdown QFE rather than the Aerodrome QFE.

SRA procedures at Coventry are designed to ICAO PANS-OPS criteria and permit descent on final approach to the OCH (in practice, to the MDH) without regard to the advisory heights given by ATC. These advisory heights are not essential for obstacle clearance and are only provided as a guide to pilots wishing to maintain a constant angle descent path. However, pilots are recommended to fly to the radar advisory heights since this will assist them in the maintenance of a stabilised approach.

1.18.6   Instrument approach charts

The CAA holds responsibility for the design of instrument approach procedures for airports within the UK, and produces approach charts as appropriate. It does not publish charts for airports in other countries. International airline operators require charts covering all of the destinations that they operate into. To meet this need, several independent chart producers present data taken from individual state sources and compile it in customised formats for subscribers.

Air Algerie operations are conducted with reference to en route and airport approach charts produced by Jeppesen, an American company which has its European subsidiary headquarters in Frankfurt, Germany. This company produces its charts on the basis of those published by the relevant state aviation authority. The details are then reproduced in a form which is compatible with the Operating Specifications laid down by the Federal Aviation Administration (FAA) in the United States. Any differences between these and the relevant state system are noted on the particular chart. Jeppesen minima show the higher of the FAA Operations Specifications or relevant state minima as appropriate.

In the Jeppesen Airway Manuals, details of instrument approach procedures are normally given on a separate page for each type of approach aid. The operating minima relevant to each aid is located on the same page.

Air Algerie aircraft are equipped with a company specified manual of approach and en route charts, covering all of the destination and alternate airports normally served by the carrier. Additionally, the manual contains specific pages detailing the approach minima for each of those airports, and these are tabulated for specific aircraft types in two weight-related classes, 2 and 3, rather than the standard A to D speed-related categorisation which has now been widely adopted in other countries.

The standard library on 7T-VEE did not include approach charts or minima for UK airfields apart from London Heathrow, London Gatwick and Manchester Airports. When the aircraft arrived at Bournemouth, it had already been specially equipped with the appropriate charts for that airport. However, when operations switched to Coventry, Phoenix Aviation provided the aircraft with a "trip kit" containing charts for airports likely to be used during the export operation.

SRAs are regarded by Jeppesen as a "final option" in the event of all of the pilot-interpreted approach aids being unavailable. As such, it is Jeppesen's stated policy not to produce a specific chart for SRA procedures in every case, unless it is the only approach aid available at a particular airport. Instead, the relevant data for SRA approaches is compiled in listing format for each country, and this is printed on separate pages and placed ahead of the individual airport chart section. However, a survey of the Jeppesen Manual showed that 31 UK airports have data presented in listing format (including Coventry), and a further 25 airports (including those which do have other approach aids available) have SRA procedures presented in the usual individual chart format.

Because of the prevalence of other types of pilot interpreted approach aids, SRA procedures are used relatively infrequently. Air Algerie crews may not have been aware of the Jeppesen policy regarding the location of the SRA approach minima data, although the Coventry Airport chart reference 11-1 (Appendix N, Figure 1) contains a note stating "FOR RADAR MINIMUMS SEE TERMINAL PAGE E-51 ETC". It is not known whether this minima page (Appendix N, Figure 2) was provided for the crew.

1.18.7   Aerodrome Operating Minima (AOM)

Certain conditions are specified in the UK for any aircraft commander who carries out, or intends to carry out, an instrument approach to a runway in conditions of low cloudbase and/or poor forward visibility. These conditions are detailed in Appendix P. There is a technical requirement for foreign operators to notify the company AOM for UK airports to the CAA. This is specified in the AIP FAL section, and the notification is required be given prior to the operation of non-scheduled commercial flights. The details of the requirement are shown in Appendix M.

The approach minima for SRAs to Runway 23 at Coventry, relevant to the Boeing 737 are:

Approach Type	Termination Range (miles)	OCH (feet)	Jeppesen MDH (feet)	Jeppesen RVR (metres)	UK PT MDH (feet)	UK PT RVR (metres)
SRA 23	2	650	655	1,500	650	1,500
SRA 23	1	370	375	1,500	370	1,100
SRA 23	0.5	370	375	1,500	370	1,100
ILS 23	n/a	310	310	1,200	310	900

There are differences between the approach minima calculated according to the provisions laid down by the CAA for UK operators, and those promulgated by Jeppesen in accordance with FAA Operations Specifications. These differences arise because the Approach Lighting System for Runway 23 at Coventry is only 416 metres in length. Under the FAA system of calculating minimum RVR, no operational credit is allowable for approaches to runways where approach lighting systems are shorter than 420 metres in length. In these cases, the RVR minimum applicable to an "Approach Lighting System Out" must be applied. Additionally, Jeppesen round up any minima calculation to the nearest 10 feet increment when first calculating MDA. The runway threshold elevation is then subtracted from this figure in order to derive the corresponding MDH. In the UK, MDH is calculated first.

Air Algerie operates scheduled passenger services into the UK, and has previously submitted details of their AOM for London Heathrow, London Gatwick and Manchester Airports, being their primary destination and weather alternate airports respectively, in accordance with this requirement.

The CAA had also previously received documentary assurance from Air Algerie, dated 29 May 1988, that their operations manual contained details of the UK Approach Ban regulation, which became effective from 1 January 1988. Details of the Approach Ban are also published in the Jeppesen Airway Manual. No details of AOM were submitted by either Air Algerie or Phoenix Aviation in respect of the 7T-VEE operations into Bournemouth, Coventry, East Midlands or Birmingham Airports. The CAA had not been informed by the DOT, Air Algerie or Phoenix Aviation that these operations were planned to take place, nor that the series of flights had in fact already commenced.

1.18.8   ATC reference to AOM

Some time before the accident, certain pilots had asked Phoenix Aviation about the exact operating minima to be applied for the SRA procedures at Coventry. Phoenix Aviation in turn requested the information from the Coventry ATSU. ATSUs do not have official reference to the MDH and RVR minima values that would normally be available, from proprietary approach charts, to pilots of aircraft on commercial flights. The only guidance promulgated in the UK AIP is that relevant to non-public transport flights by aircraft in speed category A only. A full listing of AOM for this type of flight is tabulated in the RAC section of the AIP.

For public transport operators holding a UK AOC, the criteria for calculating AOM acceptable to the CAA are detailed in CAA document CAP 360, Air Operator's Certificates. It is on these same criteria that the CAA evaluation of the acceptability of AOM submitted by foreign operators is based. This procedure in effect produces a "state minima" for each approach, but it is never referred to as such, and is not published by the CAA in the AIP. Therefore, pilots must rely on proprietary published information to indicate the appropriate minima.

Reference to aircraft types and their appropriate speed related approach categorisation is available in the AIP, but the corresponding table was withdrawn from MATS Part 1.

MATS Part 1 contains details of the standard phraseology applicable to the conduct of an SRA. In this, the pilot is informed of the termination range of the approach, and is requested to check the minima and missed approach point. No readback of the minima or missed approach point is required. The OCH is not normally passed by ATC. The practice of informing the pilot of the appropriate OCH was standard until 1991, but was then stopped. It was deleted in the interests of minimising the number of radio transmissions associated with the SRA, because it was considered that pilots would have ready access to this information on their instrument approach chart. There is a provision for the pilot to request that ATC provide the OCH, but not the MDH or minimum RVR. The OCH is therefore readily available on request.

1.18.9   Air Algerie checklists, standard operating procedures and altimetry

The checklist in use on the aircraft was an adapted version of the standard Boeing 737-200 series aircraft normal checklist. The checklist items for After Take-off, Descent-Approach and Landing are shown in Appendix R, Figure 1.

Air Algerie have the policy of conforming, as closely as possible, to the Boeing recommended operating techniques. The operating philosophy is that while in flight, the specific items are actioned from memory by the non-handling pilot, on the direction of the handling pilot. The normal checklist is then used to verify that all of the required items have been accomplished. The handling pilot is also required to instruct the non-handling pilot to action any changes of aircraft configuration (flaps, landing gear etc.). Any non-normal procedures required are conducted in accordance with the Quick Reference Handbook (QRH).

The approach briefing is carried out by the handling pilot, and should normally include details of the runway in use, the type of approach to be conducted and final approach track, the operating minima (DH or MDH, and RVR) to be observed for the approach, the settings of any required radio navigation aids, the landing flap configuration, and details of height check points relevant to the final descent. The go-around procedure should also be detailed.

Prior to the approach, the required V_{REF} and approach speeds are calculated for the actual aircraft weight, and the go-around power setting data is determined. These are recorded on a "bug card" which is positioned in view of the crew for quick reference.

Air Algerie standard operating procedures require instrument approaches to be conducted by reference to QFE. The standard operating practice with regard to altimeter cross-checking by the crew during the descent and approach phase is shown in Appendix R, Figure 2. These procedures are also an adapted version of those laid down in manufacturer's Operations Manual for the Boeing 737.

2   Analysis

2.1   General

The accident occurred during an attempt to land at Coventry after a very short flight from East Midlands Airport. The nature of the operation in which the aircraft had been engaged was controversial and had attracted considerable opposition and public protest. However, it was established at an early stage of the investigation that there was no evidence of unlawful interference with the aircraft, and the causes of the accident therefore lay purely within the bounds of aviation practice and the operation of a large jet aircraft. It was also established at an early stage that there was no evidence of aircraft or systems malfunction.

The investigation included a detailed wreckage examination and thorough analysis of the collision with the pylon. This involved matching witness marks on the pylon, houses and aircraft wreckage using computer aided design systems. This was necessary in order to establish that the aircraft had been in a normal flight attitude up to the point of impact with the pylon. Having established this fact, it was possible to eliminate possible causes such as total loss of control, uncommanded inputs to the flight controls, and system or engine failures. Pilot spatial disorientation or any external cause of the initial collision could also be ruled out.

The likely causes could be further constrained to the manner in which the aircraft had been operated and, in particular, the conduct of the Surveillance Radar Approach to Coventry. Evidence of the aircraft's flight profile was available from a combination of CVR, ATC and area radar recordings. The evidence that would have been available from a serviceable FDR, with only five basic parameters, would still not have been sufficient to determine the final flight path in terms of aircraft attitude, configuration and engine power settings. Had the other sources not been available, then lack of FDR data would have prevented a full analysis of the flight.

The task facing the crew was difficult because of poor preparation for this operation. They were operating an aircraft that was 21 years old. The avionics on board had not been updated, such that it was not possible to make use of the ILS facilities at airports such as Coventry. The only option available to them was to conduct a non-precision approach, which may be regarded as the most difficult type of approach to fly accurately. The aircraft's flight director system was to an early standard and was not capable of providing pitch commands for tracking constant vertical speed (rate of descent) during the approach. No adjustable cursors were fitted to the pressure altimeters which could have been set to indicate the proximity to the Minimum Descent Height. In addition, the final approach was to be conducted at the end of a 10 hour night duty period, when fatigue could adversely affect the crew's operational performance, such that mistakes and omissions were possible. The visibility was poor with low cloud and fog patches persisting in places. Before departure, the commander had been passed a message indicating that the weather conditions at Coventry were considerably better than those that actually existed at that time, and to compound the situation the current actual weather report and Runway Visual Range were not passed to the crew prior to the commencement of the approach. The flight time was shorter than the crew were accustomed to, and was insufficient to allow full completion of all the required tasks. The crew was not greatly experienced in the conduct of Surveillance Radar Approaches, and was not equipped with the appropriate charts to indicate the Aerodrome Operating Minima to be applied. The UK Approach Ban regulation, which should have precluded the attempted approach, was either ignored or unknown by the crew. The aircraft was offered an approach with a tail wind component, and the crew were informed that the termination range would be at 2 miles from touchdown, whereas it was continued inside that range. The aircraft did not make a stabilised approach, and descended below the advisory glidepath. This descent was not stopped at the appropriate Minimum Descent Height, even though the runway or approach lights were not visible at that time. The descent continued until the aircraft collided with the electricity pylon.

This analysis examines in detail the conduct of the final flight and the instructions passed to the crew by Air Traffic Control. Navigation and flight guidance systems are also discussed. Finally, a number of related issues including human factors, meteorological observations, ATC instructions, aerodrome Public Safety Zones and government control of foreign aircraft operations into the UK are examined.

2.2   The final flight

2.2.1   Departure, en route phase and preparation for the approach

The decision to depart from East Midlands was made on the basis of the message passed to the commander at about 0900 hrs, which indicated that the weather was 1,200 metres visibility with an overcast cloudbase at 600 feet. That cloudbase was above the MDH applicable to a 0.5 mile or 1 mile SRA termination range, and the visibility appeared to have increased towards the specified minimum quoted in the Jeppesen Manual. Given that the radiation fog was apparently starting to burn off at Coventry, it would have been reasonable for the commander to expect the conditions to further improve in the intervening period of the flight. The decision to depart immediately was therefore understandable, especially given the duty time already completed by the crew.

However, the message gave a considerably more optimistic view of the Coventry weather than was actually the case even after 0900 hrs. There is no evidence that the crew consulted the complete range of weather information that was available from the Flight Briefing Unit at East Midlands Airport before departure. This would have included the 0850 hrs METAR, which detailed considerably worse conditions than were indicated in the message to the commander.

The departure from East Midlands was normal. The direct distance from East Midlands Airport to Coventry is 34 miles, allowing for a straight-in approach track to Runway 23. Flap retraction after takeoff became delayed by radio transmissions and frequency changes. On reaching FL40, the flaps were fully retracted and the aircraft accelerated to the normal aircraft en route speed of 280 kt. In the UK, when outside controlled airspace and below FL100, a lower speed of 250 kt is mandated. Either speed would have resulted in a short flight time on this sector. The problems of very short sectors arise in completion of planning and management functions, and checklists, within the limited timescale. Sometimes approach briefings are carried out prior to takeoff, where the weather conditions and runway in use at the destination airport are available in advance. In the case of 7T-VEE, the crew did not appear to have given themselves sufficient time to complete the normal flight deck procedures that were required prior to conducting an instrument approach in marginal weather conditions.

From the evidence of the CVR (Appendix F), once the flaps had been retracted the After Take-off checklist (Appendix R, Figure 1) was completed by the commander who then immediately began reading the Descent-Approach checklist. A request by ATC to contact Birmingham Approach control interrupted the checklist flow at ALTIMETERS & INSTRUMENTS. The completion of the outstanding relevant checklist items (ALTIMETERS & INSTRUMENTS, EPR & IAS BUGS) was not heard subsequently.

Although the commander read the item APPROACH BRIEFING - REVIEWED from the checklist, no coherent discussion took place at that time, or subsequently, regarding the type of approach, how it would be conducted, nor any speeds or minima to be applied. These would normally be expected to be detailed during an approach briefing, even if completed before departure. Some short indecipherable comments were made, followed by a statement from the commander - "SET 232". This was probably a reference to setting the HSI course bars to the inbound approach track of 232° for reference. Comments and instructions by the commander, evident on the CVR, indicate that he was prompting the first officer in his handling of the aircraft. In preparation for an SRA, there is little to set up on the flight deck in terms of the navigation aids. The ADFs were tuned to the 'CT' NDB frequency, in order to give additional confirmation of centreline tracking towards the runway.

2.2.2   ATC instructions

During the early part of the approach (Appendix S, Figure 1) there was some misunderstanding by the crew of ATC instructions. When told to turn left onto a heading of 010° the acknowledgement was incorrect and the aircraft continued to fly on a heading of 100° until corrected by the controller. Also there was no positive request for the type of approach to be flown and, on the controller's own initiative, an SRA approach terminating at 2 miles from touchdown was instigated. The pilots were advised to check their minima and the missed approach point. No readback is required from the crew as to what minima and missed approach point is to be used, and none was made. In this case, the commander responded to the offer of an SRA by requesting co-operation with an SRE (sic) approach (SRE is the corresponding term used in the Jeppesen Airway Manual). This request surprised the controller, who had just passed the details of what was planned. Confirmation that an SRA to Runway 23 would be given was passed to the crew, but the termination range or check minima instruction was not reiterated. At about this time, the controller decided to continue the SRA to a termination range of 1 mile, but did not inform the crew of this, judging that there may be some difficulty with the comprehension of the change in view of the earlier exchanges with the commander. The controller did not immediately consider that the crew may need to change their operating minima for the new termination range. The commander informed the controller that the aircraft was not receiving the ILS. From the CVR evidence, there was no discussion at all between the crew about the approach being offered. These elements of confusion may be explained partly by their increasing tiredness (they had been on duty for about 10 hours), and partly by their apparently limited command of the English language.

2.2.3   Weather conditions during final approach

The current METAR and RVR for Runway 23 were not passed to the crew prior to the commencement of the final approach. Given the clear visibility above the top of the layer of fog/low stratus cloud, the crew would have had a good view of the extent of the fog around the Coventry area, and may well have been able to see ground features through gaps in the cloud cover. There was some discussion between the pilots regarding the fact that they could see the ground in patches from time to time. The commander stated that they could "COME HERE AND TRY TO GET BELOW CLOUD". Whilst the aircraft was then given further heading changes to intercept and follow the final approach track, the commander was heard on the CVR to be prompting the first officer regarding the speed, heading and aircraft configuration on occasions.

The commander said that if the approach was not successful, then they should go-around for another attempt, if they paid attention to the fuel state. At this stage, it is estimated that the aircraft had some six tonnes of fuel on board, which was quite adequate for a further approach attempt, a prolonged period of holding, and another diversion if necessary.

2.2.4   Glidepath and Minimum Descent Height

The instruction to commence the final descent was given by the controller when the aircraft was 5 miles from touchdown. The aircraft appeared to establish on the normal glidepath with a ground speed of 165 kt and with a rate of descent of about 1,100 ft/min. From about 4.1 miles inbound, the descent rate increased to an average of about 1,450 ft/min with a ground speed of 150 kt. The aircraft began to sink significantly below the normal 3° glidepath (see Appendix S, Figure 2). The selection of landing flap (30°) was probably made when the aircraft was just inside 4 miles from the runway and passing 1,100 feet, although there was no apparent completion of the landing checklist. It is most probable that the crew wanted to descend the aircraft low enough to become visual with the ground below the perceived cloudbase at an early stage during the final approach. Given the actual conditions reported in the 0950 hrs METAR and the clear skies reported above the cloud/fog layer, the initial descent below the normal glidepath would have been acceptable, if unwise in this type of aircraft, had it been stopped by the time the aircraft reached the MDH. This height should then have been maintained until the crew was visual with the runway/approach lights, or had initiated a go-around once the controller had indicated that the approach was complete. The recommended procedure, modified for large transport aircraft is described in paragraph 1.6.4, and calls for a stabilised constant glidepath towards the MDH.

The rate of descent reduced to about 750 ft/min from 2.7 miles, once the aircraft had descended below 500 feet, which was the height of the top of the cloud/fog layer noted by the pilot of the previous landing aircraft. Below this height, the rate of descent followed closely that which would have been expected for a normal approach glidepath, but the aircraft remained displaced below it and the average ground speed increased to 175 kt. Given the tailwind component of around 10 kt, the indicated airspeed at this stage of the approach would have been about 165 kt, which was considerably in excess of the correct approach speed. The maximum increment to the target V_{REF} recommended by the aircraft manufacturer is 20 kt and then only in conditions of strong and gusting winds, which was not the case here. This indicates that the flight path of the aircraft was not properly stabilised, and the handling pilot would have had to apply a great deal of attention to the aircraft's pitch attitude, power setting and airspeed in order to recover the situation and achieve a normal landing. At 1.9 miles from touchdown, the flight path descent gradient appeared to increase rapidly. There was only one further contact, at 1.8 miles from touchdown, which precluded any accurate assessment of rate of descent or ground speed. The time of the last radar contact was 0952:30.4 hrs.

A high degree of discipline between crew members is required so that the handling pilot remains continuously flying the aircraft by reference to instruments without looking outside the flight deck. The non-handling pilot (the commander in this case) also has a high workload. He is required to monitor the flight path, draw attention to any deviations from the normal flight path parameters, make the required height check calls from the altimeter indication, and to look out for the appearance of the required visual references through the obscuration. In this case, once the aircraft had descended below the nominal glidepath, the height checks being passed by the controller became superfluous, probably to the point of being intrusive and thus largely ignored by a crew who became pre-occupied with looking for ground features.

2.2.5   Decision to land or go-around

At the appropriate MDH, the non-handling pilot should call "MINIMUMS - RUNWAY IN SIGHT" or "- NO RUNWAY IN SIGHT" (Appendix R, Figure 2). Only at this stage should the handling pilot transfer his attention from the flight instruments to the outside visual references if the runway/approach lights are in sight. If they are not in sight, then a go-around must be initiated.

This final approach descent was remarkable in that there was an almost total lack of interaction between the two pilots. It was apparent during this approach that none of the standard altimeter cross-check calls were made, and that the MDH was flown through when the aircraft was still some 2.3 miles from the runway threshold. It is known from the witnesses on the industrial estate under the approach path (just inside 2 miles from touchdown) that the aircraft could be seen clearly while over the this area. It was then seen to fly into the fog bank. The crew therefore probably had some intermittently good contacts with the ground below and in front of the aircraft and so decided to continue the approach hoping that the approach lights would come into view. However, no discussion of any kind took place at this late stage of the approach.

The intentions of the pilots cannot be known for certain but, given the conditions of a thin layer of low lying stratus cloud, intermittent sightings of ground features and perhaps a strong desire to land at the base airport, there may well have been a greater desire to land rather than to go-around. It was also to be the end of a long night duty. The controller's message that the aircraft was being offered an SRA terminating at 2 miles from touchdown was not understood, and the crew may have assumed that the approach would terminate at half a mile, as it had for the earlier approach at about 0735 hrs.

The fact that the radar controller did not inform the flight crew of the decision to continue the approach inside 2 miles did not affect the resulting descent below the MDH, as the aircraft had already descended to about 300 feet by this range. Given the RVR and cloud conditions, the controller's decision to provide the aircraft with an SRA to a 1 mile termination was correct, but the flight crew should then have been informed of this fact, in order that they could have adjusted their approach minima accordingly.

The controller had no reference to actual aircraft height with the radar system in use and, not being aware that the aircraft had descended below the advisory glidepath and MDH, could not intervene to prevent the accident. In any case, responsibility for adherence to the approach profile and its minima rested solely with the crew.

2.3 Height alerting systems

2.3.1 Flight instruments

Adjustable DH/MDH cursors are fitted as standard on modern altimeters, but not to those on 7T-VEE. The cursors are normally positioned by the crew prior to an approach to indicate the applicable DH/MDH. They act as an obvious visual cue, a reminder that the minimum height is being reached. The RAs were fitted with adjustable cursors but, when these were recovered from the wreckage, they were found to be set at different settings, neither of which corresponded to any that would have been relevant to the final SRA. Thus the crew was not apparently using this facility and had no obvious reminder cues to indicate when the MDH was being passed.

Alert tones from the aural altitude alerting system were heard on the CVR at intervals during the climb and descent phases of the accident flight. None was apparent during the final approach, and the system was not designed to provide monitoring of descent progress during the final approach phase of flight.

2.3.2   Ground Proximity Warning System (GPWS)

From analysis of the radar derived height profile, it is unlikely that the Mode 1 (Excessive Descent Rate) warning would have been triggered at the calculated descent rates of the aircraft. Mode 2 (Excessive Terrain Closure Rate) alerting requires even greater closure rates than Mode 1, and would not have triggered. Mode 5 (Below Glideslope Deviation Alert) was not operative because of the lack of a valid ILS signal in this case, although it would have triggered if the aircraft had followed the accident flight profile with a serviceable and correctly tuned No 1 ILS receiver.

Mode 3 (Altitude Loss After Takeoff or Go-Around) arms when the aircraft descends below 200 feet RA in the landing configuration, and triggers if any barometric descent of more than 10 feet is sensed when the aircraft is below 700 feet RA and with the flaps in a non-landing setting (less than 30°). No "Pull Up" warning was evident, which confirmed that the flaps had not been moved up from the landing setting after the aircraft had descended through 200 feet, as would have been the case in the event of a go-around with subsequent inadvertent descent.

Mode 4 (Unsafe Terrain Clearance while not in the Landing Configuration) gives a "Pull Up" warning if the aircraft descends below 500 feet RA with the flaps not in the landing setting (30 or 40°) and the descent rate is greater than 1,450 ft/min at 500 feet RA, reducing to a trigger descent rate of 600 ft/min at 200 feet RA. This confirmed that the landing flap must have been selected while the aircraft was above about 300 feet RA.

With the aircraft in the correct landing configuration, passing over relatively flat terrain and descending within the normal range of vertical speeds on the approach, there was no warning mode available in the GPWS to indicate that the aircraft was approaching an obstacle. It was also not possible for the system to differentiate between open flat terrain and the runway surface.

2.4 Previous SRA approaches and other occurrences with 7T-VEE

The first two approaches on the day of the accident (Appendix S, Figure 3) showed close adherence to the ideal approach path; the go-around on the second approach appeared to have been initiated at MDH, at 1 mile from touchdown, despite the RTR being 0.5 mile on that occasion. The fact that both approaches were accurate indicates that the crew was capable of conducting a correctly stabilised non-precision approach in this aircraft.

Analysis was carried out on the data available from previous SRA approaches carried out by this aircraft during the month before the accident. On all 10 approaches analysed there appeared to have been little problem with centreline tracking. However, four approaches (Appendix T) showed significant displacement below the ideal glidepath throughout the approach, including one which showed gross deviation from a stabilised approach. In another case the aircraft appeared to fly level at the 1 mile MDH for a short while before it continued to descend. During all of these approaches, the aircraft apparently passed closer than usual to the top of the pylon involved in the accident. This confirms comments made by local residents about the aircraft having been observed flying very low on previous occasions.

Controllers at Coventry indicated that, on certain occasions, previous crews of 7T-VEE had caused some operational problems during the flights from Coventry. Such examples as the aircraft lining up on the active runway without ATC clearance, non-compliance with cleared altitudes after takeoff, and non-adherence to ATC navigation instructions were quoted, as well as the general complaint about the lack of an ILS on the aircraft. However, after none of these incidents did any of the controllers involved file a CAA Occurrence Report about the event. Had they done so, follow-up action by the CAA may have resulted in an assessment of the operation, and certain shortfalls in standards may have been addressed prior to the accident.

2.5 Aircraft performance aspects

Data was obtained from the Boeing Airplane Company indicating that the normal operating weights of aircraft into and out of Coventry were such that they would have complied with the UK Air Navigation (General) Regulations, in respect of takeoff and landing performance for an aircraft in Performance Group A.

The performance figures produced during the assessment indicated that the main runway at Coventry was adequate for the Boeing 737 operation. However, the margin for any inaccuracy in positioning the aircraft on the correct flight path in the final stages of the approach to land was small. Boeing's Flight Training documentation indicates that if an aircraft were to arrive over the threshold 50 feet higher than normal, then an extra 950 feet of runway would be used before the aircraft could be stopped, and a speed excess of 10 kt would use an extra 300 feet.

Therefore, it is likely that the 7T-VEE flight crews would have been concerned that the aircraft did not get too high above the normal glidepath during an approach to landing. Doing so may well have resulted in a touchdown too far past the runway threshold, thus reducing the safety margins for stopping.

2.6   ATC aspects

2.6.1   Conduct of the SRA

Little advance warning was provided to the Approach Radar controller that the aircraft was airborne from East Midlands. The handover from Birmingham afforded little time for planning. Thus the Coventry controller was without the benefit of the normal period of pre-warning associated with an IFR aircraft arriving from high level off the airways system. The aircraft was flying at a relatively higher speed than most aircraft that use Coventry Airport and the size of the radar vectoring area is small for such aircraft.

Because of the limited time available on the short sector length, the crew had not called Coventry in advance for the weather information. The controller's previous operating experience with this aircraft was that this would normally have been requested. The controller therefore adopted the 'normal routine' and believed that the current weather report had already been passed to the aircraft by the Aerodrome controller, and therefore did not pass it again. The current RVR was also assumed to have been passed with that report. This was a local working practice which was a deterioration of the correct system specified in MATS Part 1. Since the accident, local training has ensured that all Approach controllers at Coventry now broadcast the latest weather report prior to the commencement of an approach, regardless of any previous contact with the aircraft. In the absence of any voluntary provision of the weather information by the controller, the crew did not request the weather report. This is regarded as an unusual omission for pilots about to conduct an instrument approach in poor visibility.

Given the higher RVR value measured for Runway 05, and the fact that the 2,000 feet wind was from 010°/15 kt, consideration should have been given to the positioning of the aircraft for an approach to that runway. However, since the surface wind was light and any other traffic capable of using the ILS would require use of Runway 23, the decision to offer 7T-VEE an approach to that same runway was reasonable.

The initial choice of a 2 miles termination range was questionable. There is no guidance provided to Approach Radar controllers in MATS Part 1 regarding the appropriate RTRs for use in various RVR conditions. Because the RTR is quoted in miles range, and RVR is measured in metres, a calculation is involved to determine which RTR is the most appropriate.

No reference is provided for controllers on the AOM calculated in accordance with the criteria applicable to UK Public Transport operators. They cannot make a useful subjective judgement on the type of approach to offer and must rely on pilots asking for the most suitable type of approach. They cannot provide details of such AOM to pilots if it is requested. It is therefore recommended that the CAA should publish in the AIP relevant Aerodrome Operating Minima applicable to each aircraft category and type of approach, calculated in accordance with the provisions applicable to UK Public Transport Operators.
[Safety Recommendation 95-19]

2.6.2   Radio transmission phraseology

The standard phraseology for the conduct of an SRA laid down in MATS Part 1 (Appendix U) is at variance with the ICAO Procedures for Air Navigation Services (Document 4444 - RAC/501/12) in that the OCH or OCA is not passed to the crew prior to the commencement of the approach. In this accident, it is possible that the flight crew may well have been reminded in a timely manner of the OCH and in that event may not have descended the aircraft so low as to strike the pylon. Also, if the crew had been required to read back to the controller the MDH and MAPt, then the possible confusion over RTR and the correct MDH would not have occurred.

It is therefore recommended that the CAA should review the Standard Phraseology relevant to the conduct of SRA approaches which is contained in the MATS Part 1. In particular, the standard provision to pilots of the relevant Obstacle Clearance Height (or Altitude) prior to the commencement of the approach should be re-introduced, and confirmation should be sought from pilots of the Missed Approach Point and Minimum Descent Height (or Altitude) intended for use. [Safety Recommendation 95-20]

2.6.3   Aerodrome Operating Minima (AOM)

The actual AOM to be used by pilots of public transport aircraft are not published in the UK AIP. Additionally, AOM are calculated using subtly different methods by various states (see paragraph 1.18.7). In no case, however, is the MDH lower than the published OCH for the Runway and RTR in use, but the minimum RVR requirements can vary significantly, depending upon the calculation criteria.

The MDH used by the crew of 7T-VEE for the 0735 hrs approach appears to have been that relevant to the SRA terminating at 0.5 mile (or 1 mile), namely 370 feet. However, the RVR that existed at that time (advised to the crew as 700 metres) was significantly below the lowest value at which approaches are permitted under UK regulations. Either the commander was unaware of the UK regulation, had forgotten its existence, or had chosen to ignore it.

The RVR of 1,100 metres at the time of the accident would have been acceptable for an approach under UK Public Transport minima calculation criteria for this aircraft, but it was below the minimum 1,500 metres required under the FAA Specifications indicated in the Jeppesen Manual. As Air Algerie operate by reference to the Jeppesen Manuals, the final SRA appears to have contravened the UK Approach Ban regulation.

2.6.4   Enforcement of Aerodrome Operating Minima in the UK

The enforcement of the regulations pertaining to AOM is always performed retrospectively by the CAA, in cases where breaches are observed. Air Traffic Controllers are not required to be aware of the AOM to be applied and it is not within the remit of Air Traffic Controllers to decide whether or not a particular aircraft should be allowed to make an instrument approach to landing in poor weather conditions. The decision to do so is always the responsibility of the aircraft commander.

Information from the CAA indicates that there are between 20 to 30 possible infringements of the Approach Ban regulation each year, the majority of cases involving foreign operators. In many cases the breaches most likely occur because the flight crews are not aware of the UK regulations.

It is recommended that the CAA should review the current procedure whereby the UK Approach Ban regulation is notified to foreign operators, with a view to improving the method of confirmation that the content of this regulation has been disseminated to their flight crews, and that the company Aerodrome Operating Minima for UK airfields are no lower than current UK Public Transport standards. [Safety Recommendation 95-21]

2.7 Meteorological aspects

2.7.1 Provision of en route weather information

Several controllers at Coventry indicated that it was common practice at that time to pass the latest weather to an aircraft when it made its initial contact with the unit, even though at that stage it was still under the control of another ATC unit. Because the time period between the initial call and the commencement of the instrument approach, under Coventry's control, was less than the one hour time interval between METAR observations, it became local practice to only pass the weather once, at the earlier time.

At most UK airports handling significant numbers of commercial air transport movements, Meteorological observations are taken and recorded at half hourly intervals. Interspersed with these, Special Observations record intermediate changes in the weather conditions.

With the rapid changes in weather conditions that are often experienced in the UK, it is vital that pilots are kept informed of significant changes which are liable to affect the safety of the aircraft in flight, and especially when taking off or landing. Appendix L gives a summary of the observation frequency and in-flight sources of weather information available for each airport in the UK ranked in order of total numbers of Air Transport Movements for 1994.

Most airports experiencing higher traffic levels also provide the facility of an Automatic Terminal Information Service (ATIS) to provide pilots with significant operational data and the current METAR on a discrete radio frequency. This facility relieves controllers from much routine radio communication workload. It also has the added benefit that crews can obtain the information at the most convenient time with regard to flight deck workload and approach briefing considerations.

To aid pilots on longer sectors within UK airspace, weather information is also provided for a selection of the busiest airports by the VOLMET broadcast service. There are four VOLMET stations within the UK each providing weather observations, updated half hourly, for nine airports per station.

Coventry Airport does not have an ATIS facility, and is not in the VOLMET broadcast system. All weather reports to aircraft in flight have to be passed verbally by a controller.

In the case of airports such as Coventry with only hourly reporting intervals and with the lack of intermediate Special Observations during periods of high ATS workload, it is possible that vital changes in weather information may not always be available to flight crews either in flight or at the pre-flight planning stage, especially at night when ATS staff numbers are at a minimum but the number of aircraft movements can be significant.

It is therefore recommended that the CAA should ensure that weather reporting at UK airfields used for Public Transport aircraft operations be made at half hourly intervals, and disseminated accordingly. [Safety Recommendation 95-22]

2.7.2   Training of ATS Personnel in the preparation of Meteorological reports

The ATSA on duty on the morning of this accident was responsible for reporting the Meteorological observations from 0730 hrs onwards. This was his second time on duty since the completion of his Meteorological Observer certificate training course, and this was the first time that he had made observations in conditions of fog. He commented that he was still under-confident about the estimation of cloudbases, and that he had not experienced Meteorological observing in fog during his five day practical observing course at Birmingham Airport during the previous week.

Only one Meteorological Observer certificated controller was on duty prior to 0900 hrs. Acting as the Approach Radar controller for some of that time and operating the radar unit in the radar room adjacent to the VCR, it was not possible simultaneously for the controller to supervise the ATSA taking a Meteorological observation. Additionally, ATC staff had not been informed that any supervision of the newly qualified ATSA was required. A second Meteorological certificated ATCO came on duty at 0900 hrs, but he stated that he was not involved in the telephone conversation about the weather improvement at that time. Thus the supervision of this newly qualified Meteorological Observer was not adequate with the available staffing level prior to 0900 hrs, and it was unreasonable to task the newly qualified ATSA with taking Meteorological observations of weather conditions in which he had not gained supervised observing experience. It is therefore recommended that the CAA should examine the post-qualification training and supervision of newly qualified Meteorological Observers to ensure that this is adequately carried out. [Safety Recommendation 95-23]

ATCO staff who also hold Meteorological Observer Certificates and who are responsible for observations do these in addition to their normal controlling tasks. Their workload varies with the number of aircraft movements taking place and their capacity for making routine and special observations also varies accordingly.

Information from ATC staff at Coventry indicated that special observations were sometimes not taken because of the level of other workload being experienced. It was also indicated that on occasions, aircraft were passed weather observations which were different from the latest official METAR but which were observed at the time of transmission. This results in weather information being passed which is never officially recorded, as occurred with the 0900 hrs message to the accident crew.

2.8   Human factors

2.8.1   Standard of English language

The radar controller at Coventry used the correct phraseology for the conduct of the final approach, using clear and deliberate pronunciation. The crew readbacks of clearances and instructions were generally satisfactory, although there were several occasions where repetition of a message was required. On some occasions, there appeared to be a lack of understanding of the content of messages containing information which was not of a routine nature.

On two occasions during the morning of the accident, the commander had some difficulty responding to palindromic headings, 242° (readback as 224°) and 010° (understood as 100°). The latter heading was misinterpreted by both crew members while being positioned for the final approach, resulting in the aircraft flying a track 90° different from that required by the controller. This misinterpretation is considered to be an indication of crew tiredness.

The commander took over the radio transmissions from the first officer on occasions when 'non standard' conversations were taking place, and he had the better standard of spoken English. Neither of the accident crew members had been involved in any of the previous incidents at Coventry, many of which were due to a lack of understanding of the ATC messages, despite apparently correct readbacks of them.

2.8.2   Training and familiarity with SRA procedures

The SRA is regarded as a basic controller-interpreted approach aid and is usually only used when no other approach radio aids (pilot-interpreted) are available. ILS approaches are much more common. The six-monthly proficiency checks on flight crews do not require the performance of an SRA. Nevertheless, both pilots had flown successful SRAs earlier during the final duty period, each maintaining a good 3° approach path, although the approach flown by the commander resulted in a go-around as insufficient visual references existed at the end of that approach. The ambient weather conditions of temperature, pressure and wind velocity, and the weight of the aircraft, had changed little for each of the three approaches, so the aircraft power settings, pitch attitudes and airspeeds would have been similar on each occasion.

2.8.3   Effects of fatigue

Circadian rhythms of the human body can be affected when changing from day to night work. Tired pilots will have poor reaction times, an increased willingness to accept lower standards and a breakdown in instrument scanning patterns. Mistakes are made in familiar actions and attention span is decreased. Visual fields narrow, radio calls may be missed and there is often channelized attention with loss of situational awareness.

The crew involved in this accident had worked a fairly long day duty on the 19 December 1994, finishing at about 2030 hrs. Allowing for a post-flight meal and social activity, a normal night sleep duration was available to the crew members at their hotel. The following day, the crew were not required to report for duty until 2345 hrs. The activities of the crew during the day are unknown and it was not determined how much pre-duty sleep (if any) was achieved. When changing from a day duty to the first night duty in these circumstances, pilots often find difficulty achieving pre-duty sleep of any significant duration. This results in the pilots being more tired than usual at the end of the first night duty of such a sequence.

The Air Algerie FTL scheme for night duties with a maximum duty period of 7 hours 45 minutes on four sectors is more restrictive than that allowed for pilots in the UK. Even so, these schemes do not prevent pilots from becoming tired. They are primarily intended to prevent the build-up of excessive fatigue over a number of successive duties. While the actual degree of personal performance decrement due to being tired will vary for each individual but there is little doubt that a majority of pilots will feel tired following an unbroken night duty period.

FTL schemes currently consider only the time element of a duty and the number of sectors flown. There are no adjustments for ambient weather factors, or the types of approaches undertaken, both of which can add considerably to the amount of fatigue experienced by a crew during a flying duty period.

It is apparent that difficult circumstances of language, poor weather conditions, deficiencies in the aircraft's approach aids and unfamiliar approach procedures, coupled with some reduction in the level of alertness of the crew members, were all factors in this accident.

2.8.4   Possibility of visual illusions

A straight section of the A46 trunk road runs in an almost parallel direction to Runway 23 at Coventry, and the possibility that the crew may have mistaken this for the runway threshold was examined. The street lighting associated with this section of road is operated by automatic light sensing devices which would have extinguished them at about 0830 hrs on the morning of the accident, even with the presence of the foggy conditions. Because of the very poor visibility reported in the vicinity of the field in which the pylon was situated, it is unlikely that the crew would have had sufficient forward visibility to see the section of road in question.

Additionally, photographs taken on the final approach path some two miles from the threshold (Appendix H) show that if the aircraft was already low on the approach glidepath, then the relatively higher ground and trees associated with the Willenhall woodland produces a blanking effect on the approach lighting and runway threshold, making it even more difficult to locate the runway itself.

2.8.5   Crew Resource Management

Training in Crew Resource Management (CRM) includes the topics of fatigue awareness and visual illusions. ICAO Circular Human Factors No 2, 'Flight Crew Training: Cockpit Resource Management (CRM) and Line-Oriented Flight Training (LOFT)' describes this type of training, which has been progressively introduced throughout the aviation industry in recent years. In particular pilots are reminded of the adverse affects on performance that tiredness can induce and are therefore encouraged to be particularly vigilant. The possibility of encountering visual illusions of all kinds is discussed. During the training, many accident and incident scenarios are discussed, so that many may learn from the mistakes of others. Finally, CRM trained pilots are aware of the need to share high workload situations, and to monitor all the critical phases of flight so that there is back up to a single fallible human pilot. Although the first officer had received some initial training in CRM, the crew of 7T-VEE were not fully trained in these matters, and were therefore not fully prepared to cope with a most demanding situation. It is therefore recommended that Air Algerie should introduce a programme of CRM training courses for all its flight crews using the guidelines set out in ICAO-Circular-217-AN-132. [Safety Recommendation 95-24]

2.9   Permits to operate and safety standards

2.9.1   Applications for permits to operate

The one aspect of this permit application that caused the greatest confusion, and delayed processing, was the confirmation of the actual 'operator'. In terms of aircraft operational safety issues, a clear and unequivocal statement should be required as part of the permit application process about which particular company Operations Manuals and Flight Manuals are to be used for the flights. There is a requirement to provide a clear distinction between the commercial aspects of the operation and the aircraft's technical flight operation. It is also important that the identity of the aircraft operator is clearly established, so that the relevant Aerodrome Operating Minima standards may be assessed by the Safety Regulation Group of the CAA.

In the case of 7T-VEE, the aircraft remained under the direct control of Air Algerie who provided crews, maintenance and operational procedures. Therefore, it is the Air Algerie AOC which should have represented the 'Certificate of Competency'. The use of another airline's name, callsign and flight number designator for flight planning or commercial purposes is irrelevant to the safe conduct of the flights. In this case Race Cargo Airlines had no input whatsoever to the actual operation of this aircraft.

It is therefore recommended that the Department of Transport, International Aviation Directorate, in conjunction with the CAA, should review the current Permit application system, and the requirements detailed in the UK AIP. A standard Permit application and approval scheme should be devised to ensure compliance with the requirements of the FAL section of the AIP and that this be confirmed prior to the commencement of the proposed flights. For the purposes of Permit applications, the applicant should be required to submit a clear statement as to which Airline Operations Manuals and Flight Manuals will be applicable to the proposed operations, and the current documentary requirements should be based upon this information. [Safety Recommendation 95-25]

2.9.2   The Chicago Convention and ICAO Standards and Recommended Practices

Because of the obligations placed on the UK by Article 33 of the Convention on International Civil Aviation (see paragraph 1.18.4), it is likely that the required DOT permits would have been issued in due course to authorise the operations from Coventry, but the occurrence of the accident suspended the processing procedure. It is unlikely that the incompatibility between the aircraft ILS receivers and the Coventry ILS would have been detected by this application process, because it is intended simply to establish that the documentation in respect of the subject aircraft and operator conforms to the ICAO Standards and Recommended Practices (SARPs) referred to in Article 33. Whilst there is no bar to the physical confirmation of the airworthiness of the aircraft or the actual standards laid down for its operation, it is not compatible with the obligations of Article 33 for acceptance of foreign operators' certificates to be refused. Where there is evidence that minimum ICAO standards have not been met, then permits may be refused. Such evidence is unlikely to come to light in the absence of any safety oversight by the issuing authority. Accident prevention measures require a proactive programme to discover real and potential safety deficiencies before they lead to an accident. Recognising this, one major State has already begun to check certain airworthiness matters involving foreign operators with air service agreements or permits to operate. ICAO itself initiated in August 1995 a safety oversight programme which is intended to assist States to obtain outside support for safety oversight. The programme's main function is to perform oversight assessments of States on a voluntary basis, with the objective of identifying deficiencies and offering advice and assistance in addressing problem areas so that States are able to implement ICAO SARPs and associated procedures. These are welcome initiatives and, subject to their successful implementation on a global basis, pre-empt the safety recommendation that this investigation would otherwise have made.

2.10 Management of Air Algerie Flight Operations

2.10.1 Flight Safety Organisation

This aircraft was operating from Coventry for a number of weeks with a navigation receiver system which was incompatible with the Coventry ILS frequency. This was well known by the pilots and the charterer. The deficiency had been reported to the Air Algerie Flight Operations Department, but no remedial action had been taken. Had the flight crews reported this problem through a company Flight Safety Organisation at an early stage, it is possible that rectification action could have been introduced earlier. This would have removed the necessity for the accident crew to have performed a non-precision approach on the morning of the accident. It is therefore recommended that Air Algerie should introduce a Flight Safety Management function within its Operations Department. [Safety Recommendation 95-26]

2.10.2 Monitoring of Air Algerie Operating Standards

The current situation, where selected Captains within Air Algerie are tasked with monitoring the flight operating standards of the company on behalf of the Algerian Department of Civil Aviation does not provide a fully independent monitoring and auditing function. It is therefore recommended that the Algerian Department of Civil Aviation should review its policy for monitoring the operating standards of Air Algerie, with a view to providing a more independent assessment of the standards being attained. [Safety Recommendation 95-27]

3   Conclusions

(a)   Findings

The aircraft

1   The aircraft had been maintained and was serviceable with no significant defects. There was no evidence of unlawful interference with the aircraft.

2   The aircraft did not suffer any systems failures or malfunctions during its final flight which would have caused the collision with the pylon.

3   The estimated weight and loading of the aircraft were within the normal operating limits at the time of the accident. There was sufficient fuel on board to conduct the approach, go-around, hold and then to divert if necessary.

4   The aircraft was unable to receive the Coventry ILS because it was fitted with an ILS receiver which was incompatible with the Coventry ILS frequencies. Therefore there was no precision approach system available at Coventry for use by this aircraft. In order to land there the crew had to use a non-precision instrument approach procedure.

5   Since the aircraft was in the correct landing configuration and descending on approach at normal descent rates over relatively flat terrain, the Ground Proximity Warning System, by its design, could not provide a warning to the crew that the aircraft was too low.

6   The aircraft's pressure altimeters were not fitted with any adjustable cursor which could have been set to indicate the Minimum Descent Height for the approach being carried out. Radio altimeter cursors were available but did not appear to have been set appropriately by the crew.

The crew

7   The crew was properly licensed and medically fit to conduct the flight.

8   The pre-flight rest period in excess of 27 hours was adequate. The flight duty period at the time of the accident was just over 10 hours, which was more than 2 hours in excess of the operator's normal maximum for night duties. Five sectors were operated by the crew but the operator's flight time limitation scheme allowed this under exceptional circumstances, such as a weather diversion.

66

9   The commander based his decision to operate the flight from East Midlands to Coventry on an incorrect assessment of the existing weather conditions at Coventry that was passed to him at about 0900 hrs.

10   Because the duration of the final flight was unusually short, the crew found themselves with insufficient time to complete all of the normal flight deck procedures.

11   There was little evidence of consultation between the commander and first officer regarding the proposed conduct of the SRA and its approach minima. During the approach, there was a marked lack of interaction between the two pilots. The landing checklist was not completed, and there was no cross-checking of the altimeter indications.

12   Because of the nature of the fog or low stratus cloud, the crew would have seen the ground intermittently, and both of them were probably looking for the required visual references to land.

13   The aircraft's flight path was not stabilised during the final approach, and the airspeed became excessive.

14   The fact that the crew had been on duty for such a long period would have given them a strong incentive to land at Coventry and terminate their duty.

15   Limited comprehension of the English language made the conduct of the SRA more difficult, and fatigue would have reduced their level of alertness.

16   It is unlikely that the crew would have seen the pylon in sufficient time to take avoiding action. With the aircraft so low on the approach, the runway threshold and approach lighting would have been obscured by intervening woodland and terrain. The A46 trunk road would have been obscured by the poor visibility at the particular location.

17   The crew had earlier demonstrated their ability to conduct a correctly stabilised SRA approach, and to execute a go-around on reaching the Minimum Descent Height.

18   Given the Landing Distance Available at Coventry, the crew would have been concerned not to land too far past the threshold with a consequent reduction in the safety margin for stopping.

19   In the absence of any voluntary provision of weather information by ATC, the crew did not request the weather report or Runway Visual Range. This was an unusual omission for a crew about to conduct an instrument approach in poor visibility.

Air Traffic Control

20   The Approach and Approach Radar controller was properly licensed, medically fit and correctly rated to provide the service.

21   All of the aerodrome approach aids and lighting facilities were serviceable at the time of the accident.

22   The standard operating procedure of passing the current weather and RVR to the aircraft prior to the commencement of an instrument approach was not complied with.

23   The controller's decision to offer the aircraft an SRA to Runway 23, despite the fact that there was better visibility on Runway 05, was reasonable given the light surface wind and other traffic considerations.

24   The controller appreciated the difficulties facing the crew, including the fact that the aircraft was unable to receive the ILS, and relative difficulty in following instructions in English. The SRA to Runway 23 was conducted correctly, using the standard phraseology detailed in MATS Part 1. The crew had been informed that the approach would terminate at 2 miles from touchdown, but the controller should have declared the subsequent decision to continue the approach guidance to a 1 mile termination range.

25   The radar systems at Coventry have no facility for indicating the actual height of the aircraft relative to the advisory glidepath. The controller could not have been aware that the aircraft descended below the advisory glidepath, or that it had flown below the Obstacle Clearance Height and was therefore not in a position to have warned the crew or prevented the accident.

26   The crew was not advised of the appropriate OCH as it was not the standard practice for ATC to pass this information unless requested. Had the requirement existed for ATC to advise the appropriate OCH prior to the approach, and had the crew been required to read back their MDH and Missed Approach Point, then they would have had the benefit of a timely reminder of these vital items.

68

27   Supervision of the newly qualified ATSA Meteorological observer on duty in the ATSU at Coventry was inadequate. The ATSA had never before been responsible for taking observations in conditions of fog or lifting fog. Standard procedures, set out in MATS Part 1, were not followed such that an updated Special observation was not taken when the weather conditions began to improve.

28   The recording of Special Meteorological observations at Coventry, and the provision of Meteorological information to aircraft, were not always carried out in accordance with the standard procedures. This resulted in a lack of reporting of significant changes in the weather conditions, and information was passed to aircraft that had never been officially recorded.

29   Meteorological observations at Coventry Airport were made hourly. In the prevailing conditions of lifting low stratus cloud and dispersing fog more frequent updates were required so that pilots could be given the latest information.

The operation

30   The SRA approaches conducted at 0735 hrs and at the time of the accident contravened the UK Approach Ban regulation because the RVR was insufficient. The crew may have been unaware of the regulation.

31   The crew had not been fully trained in all aspects of Crew Resource Management. If they had been they would have been more aware of the effect of tiredness on their individual performances and judgements with the attendant need for close and mutual monitoring.

32   Several operational errors were made during the aircraft's period of operation from Coventry, but these were not officially reported and no supervisory action was taken.

33   The series of flights, for the purpose of live animal exports, did not have the required Permits issued by the Department of Transport, International Aviation Directorate.

34   There was no Flight Safety organisation within Air Algerie which could have acted as a direct reporting channel, through which crews could express their concerns about the operation of the aircraft.

35   There was no independent checking of the flight operations standards within Air Algerie because the task is delegated, by the Algerian Department of Civil Aviation, to senior Captains within the company.

(b)   **Causes**

The following causal factors were identified:

i)   The flight crew allowed the aircraft to descend significantly below the normal approach glidepath during a Surveillance Radar Approach to Runway 23 at Coventry Airport, in conditions of patchy lifting fog. The descent was continued below the promulgated Minimum Descent Height without the appropriate visual reference to the approach lighting or the runway threshold.

ii)   The standard company operating procedure of cross-checking altimeter height indications during the approach was not observed and the appropriate Minimum Descent Height was not called by the non-handling pilot.

iii)   The performance of the flight crew was impaired by, the effects of tiredness having completed over 10 hours of flight duty through the night, during five flight sectors which included a total of six approaches to land.

4   Safety Recommendations

The following safety recommendations are made:

4.1   The CAA should publish in the AIP relevant Aerodrome Operating Minima applicable to each aircraft category and type of approach, calculated in accordance with the provisions applicable to UK Public Transport Operators. [Safety Recommendation 95-19]

4.2   The CAA should review the Standard Phraseology relevant to the conduct of SRA approaches which is contained in the MATS Part 1. Consideration should be given to the re-introduction of the standard provision to pilots of the relevant Obstacle Clearance Height (or Altitude) prior to the commencement of the approach and that confirmation should be sought from pilots of the Missed Approach Point and Minimum Descent Height (or Altitude) intended for use.
[Safety Recommendation 95-20]

4.3   The CAA should review the current procedure whereby the UK Approach Ban regulation is notified to foreign operators, with a view to improving the method of confirmation that the content of this regulation has been disseminated to their flight crews, and that the company Aerodrome Operating Minima for UK airfields are no lower than current UK Public Transport standards. [Safety Recommendation 95-21]

4.4   The CAA should ensure that weather reporting at UK airfields used for Public Transport aircraft operations be made at half hourly intervals, and disseminated accordingly. [Safety Recommendation 95-22]

4.5   The CAA should examine the post-qualification training and supervision of newly qualified Meteorological Observers to ensure that this is adequately carried out. [Safety Recommendation 95-23]

4.6   Air Algerie should introduce a programme of CRM training courses for all its flight crews using the guidelines set out in ICAO Circular 217-AN132. [Safety Recommendation 95-24]

4.7   The Department of Transport, International Aviation Directorate, in conjunction with the CAA, should review the current Permit application system, and the requirements detailed in the UK AIP. A standardised

Permit application and approval scheme should be devised to ensure compliance with the requirements of the FAL section of the AIP. This should be confirmed prior to the commencement of the proposed flights. For the purposes of Permit applications, the applicant should be required to submit a clear statement as to which Airline Operations Manuals and Flight Manuals will be applicable to the proposed operations, and the current documentary requirements should be based upon this information. [Safety Recommendation 95-25]

4.8   Air Algerie should introduce a Flight Safety Management function within its Operations Department. [Safety Recommendation 95-26]

4.9   The Algerian Civil Aviation Department should review its policy for monitoring the operating standards of Air Algerie, with a view to providing a more independent assessment of the standards being attained. [Safety Recommendation 95-27]

R StJ Whidborne
Inspector of Air Accidents
Air Accidents Investigation Branch
Department of Transport

December 1995

BOEING 737
OPERATIONS MANUAL

APPROACH PROCEDURE

Flap Extension

Using flaps as speedbrakes is not recommended.

The following procedures and maneuvering speeds are used for extending flaps:

NORMAL MANEUVER AND FLAP EXTENSION SPEEDS		
FLAP POS	NORMAL MANEUVER	SELECT FLAP
0	210	1
1	190	5
5	170	15
*10	160	15
15	150/VREF	25
25	140	30-40

*Used only during one engine inoperative non-precision approaches or one engine inoperative circling approach.

Approach

For a normal approach, the landing configuration (gear down and landing flaps) is established early on final approach.

Stabilize on speed and profile with airplane in trim.

A normal profile of 2.5 to 3 degrees results in a descent of 500 to 800 feet per minute, which is the same as for a standard ILS.

High, low, or offset corrections should be made as early in the approach as possible, in order to be in a stabilized condition through the last 500 feet of the approach.

The pilot should maintain a constant profile and proper rate of descent coordinating pitch attitude with power changes.

Approach Speed

The Boeing recommended approach speed wind correction is 1/2 the steady headwind component plus all of the gust value, based on tower reported winds. The maximum wind correction should not normally exceed 20 knots. In all cases, the gust correction should be maintained to touchdown while the steady wind correction should be bled off as the airplane approaches touchdown.

When the wind is reported calm or light and variable, and no windshear exists, VREF + 5 knots is the recommended airspeed on final, bleeding off the 5 knots as the aircraft approaches touchdown. If this normal 5 knots is being carried above VREF on final approach, do not add any additional speed for a headwind component of up to 10 knots.

Do not apply a wind correction on final approach speed (VREF) for tail winds.

Example

Headwind component = 18 knots, gusting 25 knots. Add 9 knots for headwind component and 7 knots for gust effect, resulting in an approach speed equal to VREF + 16 knots.

OPERATIONS MANUAL

APPROACH PROCEDURE (Cont)

Non Precision Approach

When making a VOR or ADF approach,
descend to Minimum Descent Altitude
(MDA) as soon as practical after
passing the final fix inbound. Just
prior to starting descent, extend flaps
to the final landing flap setting and
reduce speed to approach speed. If a
circling approach is planned, it is
recommended to maintain flaps 15 and
flaps 15 maneuvering speed until
selecting final flap setting just prior
to turning base on final approach.

The pilot should not dive at the runway
when breaking clear of clouds at low
altitudes from an instrument approach.
High rates of descent that develop with
this maneuver are not readily apparent
on either the Airspeed Indicator or the
Vertical Speed Indicator, and may not
be noticed until the flare point.

Crosswind

The crab, sideslip, or a combination of
both are accepted methods of correcting
for a crosswind during approach and
landing. Regardless of which method is
used, there is sufficient rudder and
aileron control available to execute
crosswind landings.

Landing

As the airplane approaches the
touchdown point, reduce descent rate,
smoothly retard thrust to IDLE and
maintain the flight profile to
touchdown. Use speedbrakes, brakes,
and reverse thrust normally after
touchdown.

The First Officer should check the
speedbrake full up.

In the event of a bounced landing, hold
or re-establish normal landing
attitude. Add thrust as necessary to
control the sink rate. Do not push
over, as this may cause a second bounce
and possibly damage the nose gear.

Use rudder to hold the airplane on
centerline. Displacing the aileron
into the wind assists in directional
control. Nose wheel steering improves
with forward pressure on the control
column which increases weight on the
nose gear. The aileron and rudder
controls are effective down to
approximately 50 knots.

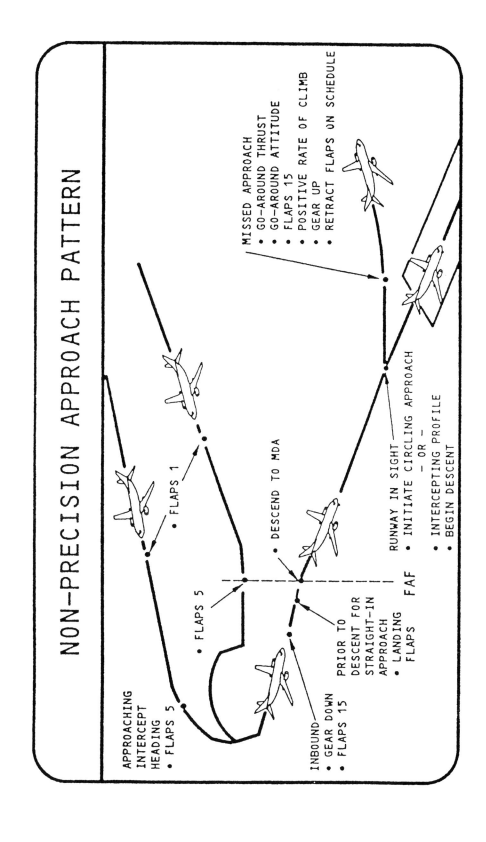

BOEING 737
OPERATIONS MANUAL

NON-PRECISION APPROACH PATTERN

APPROACHING
INTERCEPT
HEADING
• FLAPS 5

• FLAPS 1

• FLAPS 5

• DESCEND TO MDA

PRIOR TO
DESCENT FOR
STRAIGHT-IN
APPROACH
• LANDING
  FLAPS

INBOUND
• GEAR DOWN
• FLAPS 15

FAF

RUNWAY IN SIGHT
• INITIATE CIRCLING APPROACH
  – OR –
• INTERCEPTING PROFILE
• BEGIN DESCENT

MISSED APPROACH
• GO-AROUND THRUST
• GO-AROUND ATTITUDE
• FLAPS 15
• POSITIVE RATE OF CLIMB
• GEAR UP
• RETRACT FLAPS ON SCHEDULE

METARs

TIME	SURFACE WIND	VISIBILITY (metres)	WEATHER	CLOUD1 (base in feet agl)	CLOUD2 (base in feet agl)	TEMP °C	QNH (mb)
0650	350/04	800	FOG	OVERCAST 100	-	2	1021
0750	040/04	300	FOG	OVERCAST 100	-	1	1022
0850	CALM	500	FOG	OVERCAST 100	-	2	1023
0950	020/06	1,200	MIST	SCATTERED 700	SCATTERED 1,200	2	1023

RVRs

TIME	RWY 05 (metres)	RWY 23 (metres)
0632	-	1,000
0655	-	800
0734	-	700
0740	-	700
0743	-	600
0750	-	600
0753	550	-
0841	-	450
0844	600	-
0853	800	-
0904	-	900
0916	-	1,000
0925	-	900
0927	900	-
0933	1,200	-
0940	>1,300	-
0945	-	1,100

ROUTINE WEATHER REPORTS AND RUNWAY VISUAL RANGE MEASUREMENTS COVENTRY AIRPORT - 21 DECEMBER 1994

➡ 5   **AERODROME METEOROLOGICAL REPORTS (SPECIAL)**

Specific improvements and deteriorations of any of the items in a routine report are supplied in a special report. They are issued between routine reports and contain only those items which are affected. The criteria for raising special reports are shown in the table below.

Surface Wind	*Criteria agreed locally. (Only issued when there is not a wind indicator in the control tower.)*
Surface Visibility	Increases and decreases to, or through: 800 metres 5000 metres 1500 metres 10 kilometres In addition arrangements can be made at aerodromes where RVR is not available, either permanently or during a temporary unserviceability, to report increases and decreases to, or through: 150 metres 350 metres 600 metres
Weather	At the onset, cessation or change in intensity of: Moderate or heavy: rain, rain and snow mixed, hail, snow pellets or ice pellets Freezing precipitation Thunderstorm Funnel cloud (tornado or waterspout) Squall Low drifting or blowing; snow, dust or Dust or sandstorm sand
Cloud	Base: When the base of the lowest cloud covering more than half the sky increases or decreases to, or through: 2000 feet 500 feet 1500 feet 300 feet 1000 feet 200 feet 700 feet 100 feet At certain aerodromes the upper limit may be higher. Amount: When the amount of the lowest layer at or below 1500 feet changes from half or less to more than half; and vice versa.
Pressure	When the QNH or QFE changes by 1·0 millibar.
Severe icing and/or turbulence	When an aircraft on the approach or on climb out reports severe icing and/or severe turbulence, and it is confirmed by the duty forecaster at the local meteorological forecast office.

RADAR VECTORING AREA

COVENTRY

	Elevation 281ft	Transition Alt 3000ft

GENERAL INFORMATION
1. All bearings are magnetic.
2. Levels shown are based on QNH.
3. Only significant obstacles and dominant spot heights are shown.
4. The minimum levels shown within the Radar Vectoring Area ensure terrain clearance in conformity with Rule 29 of the Rules of the Air Regulations in respect of obstacles within the RVA.
5. Minimum Sector Altitudes are based on obstacles and spot heights within 25NM of the Aerodrome Reference Point.

Within the Radar Vectoring Area the minimum initial altitude to be allocated by the radar controller is 1700ft. Descent below 1700ft may be given within the SRA Final Approach Area when on 40° leg or Final Approach.

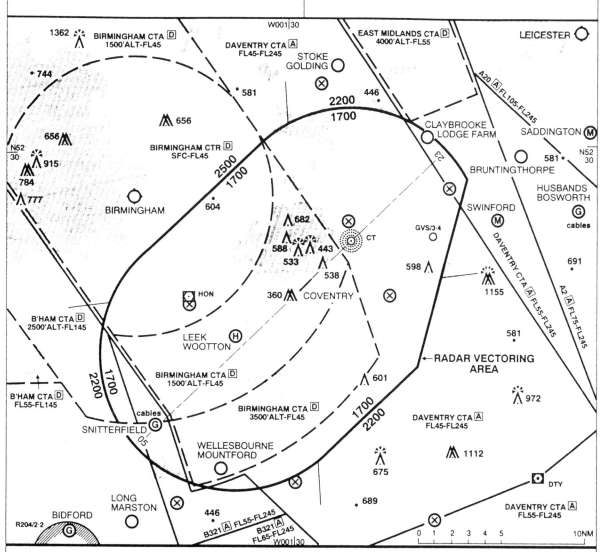

LOSS OF COMMUNICATION PROCEDURES

Initial and Intermediate Approach
Continue visually remaining outside Birmingham CTA and CTR or by means of an appropriate final approach aid. If not possible proceed at 2500ft, or last assigned level if higher, (but not above 1500ft untill clear of Birmingham CTA) to CT NDB*.

Within Final Approach Area
Continue visually or by means of an appropriate final approach aid. If not possible follow the Missed Approach Procedure to CT NDB*

* In all cases where the aircraft returns to the holding facility the procedure to be adopted is the basic Radio Failure Procedure detailed at RAC 6.

4·2·94

INSTRUMENT
APPROACH
CHART – ICAO

N52 22.16
W001 28.69

ELEV 281FT

VAR 5°W

BEARINGS ARE MAGNETIC
ELEVATIONS IN FEET AMSL 682
HEIGHTS IN FEET ABOVE
THR ELEV RWY 23 .... (417)

ACFT
CAT
A,B,C,D

RADIO

RAD	122.00	COVENTRY RADAR
VDF	122.00, 119.25, 124.80	COVENTRY APPROACH, TOWER, RADAR (Not en-route)
APP	119.25	COVENTRY APPROACH
TWR	119.25, 124.80, 121.70 (GMC)	COVENTRY TOWER / COVENTRY GROUND

LIGHTING

IBN	Flashing green CT
APP 05	426m HI C/L 1 bar. PAPI (3°) LHS.
23	416m HI C/L 2 bar. PAPI (3°) LHS.
THR 05	Elev HI green W bars
23	HI green with elev HI green W bars.
RWY 05/23	Elev HI bi-d with LI omni-d component. End lights red Red edge to grass stopway.
TWY	Green C/L from main apron to Hold A. Blue edge from N Airpark to Hold K.

MISSED APPROACH POINT

MISSED APPROACH POINT 1   SRA RTR 0.5NM
MISSED APPROACH POINT 2   SRA RTR 1NM
MISSED APPROACH POINT 3   SRA RTR 2NM

MISSED APPROACH PROCEDURE

At or before the Missed Approach Point climb straight ahead to 1266(1000) then climbing turn left onto 160°M to 1500(1234). Turn to intercept and track inbound the VOR DTY R305 (VOR HON R125). When at DTY DME 14 or less (HON DME 9 or more) continue climb to 2000ALT then turn left to return to NDB CT or as directed by ATC.

OBSTACLE CLEARANCE ALTITUDE/HEIGHT

AIRCRAFT CATEGORY	A	B	C	D
SRA RTR 0.5NM	636(370)	636(370)	636(370)	636(370)
SRA RTR 1NM	636(370)	636(370)	636(370)	636(370)
SRA RTR 2NM	916(650)	916(650)	916(650)	916(650)
VISUAL MANOEUVRING	881(600)†	931(650)†	1131(850)†	1131(850)†

† Heights in feet AAL

LOWEST ALTITUDE   2000 for holding

MAXIMUM IAS   HOLD 170KT

NOTE   When using VOR DTY some receivers may show abnormal characteristics

RADAR APPROACH PROCEDURE (Nominal approach slope 3°)

RANGE FROM TOUCHDOWN	NM	4.5	4.0	3.5	3.0	2.5	2.0	1.5	1.0
ADVISORY HEIGHT	FT	1400	1250	1100	950	800	650	500	350

CHANGE   NEW RTR 1NM/2NM PROCEDURES

© CIVIL AVIATION AUTHORITY 1994
WHOSE PERMISSION MUST BE OBTAINED
BEFORE THIS CHART IS REPRODUCED

SHEET 2750

MNM SECT ALT 2200 25NM
MNM SECT ALT 2500 25NM
MNM SECT ALT 2200 25NM
MNM SECT ALT 2200 25NM

Transition Altitude 3000

CLAYBROOKE LODGE FARM
BRUNTINGTHORPE   cables
SWINFORD

STOKE GOLDING

COVENTRY CT 363.5

BIRMINGHAM CTR SFC-FL45
BIRMINGHAM

HONILEY HON 113.65

LEEK WOOTTON
BIRMINGHAM CTA 1500ALT-FL45

SNITTERFIELD   cables

GVS SFC-3400ALT

COVENTRY SRA RTR 0.5NM/1NM/2NM RWY 23

FAF
FAF   4.5NM radar range
Not below 1665 (1400)
NDB CT
MAPT
DTY VOR R305
DTY D14
DTY D14 (or less)
DTY VOR R305

Climbing turn left
Turn left
2000
1500
1265 (1000)

QFE DATUM 265 (THR ELEV RWY 23)

Initial and Intermediate Approach as directed by radar

PUBLISHED BY THE CIVIL AVIATION AUTHORITY

AERO INFO DATE 31 Mar 94

D-2

Runway Primary Aids FAT °MAG	Procedures	Aircraft Categories OCH (ft)	Missed Approach Procedure
Coventry Runway 23 † SRA - RTR 0.5 nm 232°	**Nominal Glidepath 3°** Initial and intermediate approach as directed by radar. From FAF (4.5 nm radar range) not below **1665** (1400) ft, follow nominal glidepath advisory heights to MDH. Nominal Final Approach Gradient 4.9%, 300 ft/nm.	A/B/C/D 370	At or before MAPt (RTR 0.5 nm), climb straight ahead to **1265** (1000) ft, then climbing turn left onto track 160° MAG to **1500** (1235) ft. Turn to intercept and track inbound the VOR DTY 305 radial (VOR HON 125 radial). When at 14 DME DTY or less (9 DME HON or more), continue climb to **2000** ft, then turn left to return to NDB(L) CT, or as directed by ATC.
Coventry Runway 23 † SRA - RTR 1 nm 232°	**Nominal Glidepath 3°** Initial and intermediate approach as directed by radar. From FAF (5 nm radar range) not below **1815** (1550) ft, follow nominal glidepath advisory heights to MDH. Nominal Final Approach Gradient 4.9%, 300 ft/nm.	A/B/C/D 370	At or before MAPt (RTR 1 nm), climb straight ahead to **1265** (1000) ft, then climbing turn left onto track 160° MAG to **1500** (1235) ft. Turn to intercept and track inbound the VOR DTY 305 radial (VOR HON 125 radial). When at 14 DME DTY or less (9 DME HON or more), continue climb to **2000** ft, then turn left to return to NDB(L) CT, or as directed by ATC.
Coventry Runway 23 † SRA - RTR 2 nm 232°	**Nominal Glidepath 3°** Initial and intermediate approach as directed by radar. From FAF (5 nm radar range) not below **1815** (1550) ft, follow nominal glidepath advisory heights to MDH. Nominal Final Approach Gradient 4.9%, 300 ft/nm.	A/B/C/D 650	At or before MAPt (RTR 2 nm), climb straight ahead to **1265** (1000) ft, then climbing turn left onto track 160° MAG to **1500** (1235) ft. Turn to intercept and track inbound the VOR DTY 305 radial (VOR HON 125 radial). When at 14 DME DTY or less (9 DME HON or more), continue climb to **2000** ft, then turn left to return to NDB(L) CT, or as directed by ATC.
Coventry Runway 23 † VDF 225°	**Aircraft Categories A and B only:** Arrival not below MSA **(Note)**; Shuttle as required. Overhead VDF, fly outbound on QDR 205° (QDM 025°) for 2.5 minutes descending to **1565** (1300) ft. Base turn left onto FAT. **Shuttle Procedure:** Overhead VDF, fly outbound on QDR 205° (QDM 025°) for 1-minute, turning right onto QDM 063° to return to the facility. **Note:** Minimum altitude within 10 nm of VDF facility **1700** ft. FAT is off-set by 7° from Runway centre-line and nominal intercept occurs 1.2 nm before threshold.	A/B 570	At MAPt (VDF overhead), climb straight ahead to **1265** (1000) ft, then climbing turn left onto track 160° MAG to **1500** (1235) ft, then continue as directed by ATC.

D-3

THE TRAINING OF AIR TRAFFIC SERVICES PERSONNEL IN THE PREPARATION OF AERODROME WEATHER REPORTS

CAA Aeronautical Information Circular number 62/1994 (White 184) gives details of the Training of Air Traffic Services Personnel in the Preparation of Aerodrome Weather Reports. The relevant extracts are:

1. Aerodrome weather reports made by ATS personnel at UK aerodromes and provided to aircraft will not be accepted by the CAA as METAR for dissemination beyond the aerodrome on the AFTN, OPMET or VOLMET unless the reports are compiled by a qualified meteorological observer. Furthermore, only reports from qualified observers will be used as the basis for the production of TAF by the parent Met Office. It is therefore essential that the ATS personnel concerned have received appropriate training to become accredited observers.

2. The Meteorological Office, on behalf of the CAA, arranges the necessary courses of training in meteorological observation and reporting for ATS personnel. A copy of the syllabus is shown at Annex A circular 62/1994.

3. The courses consist of five days spent residentially at the Meteorological Office College, followed by a further week of practical training (including night time observations) at a Meteorological Office unit. Examinations are set at the end of each week of the course and candidates who successfully complete the two week course will receive a certificate to that effect. Holders of a certificate become accredited observers for the purposes of the MATS Part 1, Section 7, Chapter 1, paragraph 3(f).

4. On completion of the formal Met Office training, the responsibility for ensuring that certificated observers fulfil their weather reporting duties satisfactorily is that of the aerodrome management, usually the Air Traffic Control Manager/SATCO. Although two weeks of professional training is the minimum required for the award of a certificate, no newly certificated observer can be considered competent or fully qualified without a period of further 'on the job' training at his/her home aerodrome under the supervision of more experienced colleagues/observers and in a variety of weather situations.

TIME GMT	TIME TO END	FROM	TO	RTF COMMUNICATION	ORIGIN	FLIGHT DECK COMMUNICATION	REMARKS
				EXTRACT BEGINS		**NOTE: BRACKETS DENOTE UNCERTAIN WORDS ITALICS DENOTE TRANSLATION FROM FRENCH OR ARABIC**	
9:36	16:25	EAST MID TWR	702P	SEVEN ZERO TWO PAPA - ER - AFTER DEPARTURE YOU'RE CLEARED TO LEAVE THE ZONE CLIMBING STRAIGHT AHEAD TO FLIGHT LEVEL FOUR ZERO THE SQUAWK SEVEN THREE SIX FIVE			
		702P	EAST MID TWR	STRAIGHT AHEAD CLIMBING FLIGHT LEVEL FOUR ZERO SQUAWKING SEVEN THREE SIX FIVE			
		EAST MID TWR	702P	PAPA THAT'S CORRECT IT WILL BE STRAIGHT AHEAD AND AFTER THE LANDING D C NINE LINE UP TWO SEVEN			
		702P	EAST MID TWR	AFTER THE LANDING AIRCRAFT WE LINE UP SEVEN ZERO TWO PAPA			
				EXTRACT ENDS			

TIME GMT	TIME TO END	FROM	TO	RTF COMMUNICATION	ORIGIN	FLIGHT DECK COMMUNICATION	REMARKS
9:37	15:40	EAST MID TWR	702P	**EXTRACT BEGINS** SEVEN ZERO TWO PAPA LINE UP TWO SEVEN			
		702P	EAST MID TWR	LINE UP SEVEN ZERO TWO PAPA **EXTRACT ENDS**			
				EXTRACT BEGINS			
	15:07	EAST MID TWR	702P	SEVEN ZERO TWO PAPA CLIMBING STRAIGHT AHEAD CLEARED TAKE OFF WIND NORTHERLY THREE			
		702P	EMT	CLEAR TAKE OFF CLIMBING STRAIGHT AHEAD SEVEN ZERO TWO PAPA	P1	CLEAR TAKE OFF LIGHTS - TRANSPONDER ON	
					P2	?	

TIME GMT	TIME TO END	FROM	TO	RTF COMMUNICATION	ORIGIN	FLIGHT DECK COMMUNICATION	REMARKS
9:38					P1	(LEFT)	SOUND OF ENGINE RUN-UP FOR TAKE-OFF N1=90% (POWER LEVELS HAVE BEEN DERIVED FROM AREA MICROPHONE DUE TO TAPE SPEED VARIATIONS ACCURACY ±5%)
					P2	(POWER)	
					P1	SPEED'S RISING	
					P1	ENGINE DATA GREEN	
					P1	EIGHTY KNOTS	
					P1	V ONE VR	
					P1	POSITIVE RATE	
					P2	CHECK GEAR UP	
	14:29			EXTRACT ENDS			
					P2	CLIMB THRUST	
	14:00			EXTRACT BEGINS			
	13:58	EAST MID TWR	702P	SEVEN ZERO TWO PAPA YOU CAN TURN LEFT NOW ON COURSE CHARLIE TANGO			
		702P	EAST MID TWR	TURN LEFT ON COURSE TO CHARLIE - CHARLIE TANGO	P2	(SET CHARLIE TANGO)	
					P1	HEADING ONE EIGHT ZERO	

TIME GMT	TIME TO END	RTF COMMUNICATION FROM	TO	RTF COMMUNICATION	FLIGHT DECK COMMUNICATION ORIGIN	FLIGHT DECK COMMUNICATION	REMARKS
9:39	13:38	EAST MID TWR	702P	SEVEN ZERO TWO PAPA CONTACT EAST MIDLANDS APPROACH ONE ONE NINE DECIMAL SIX FIVE			ALT ALERT
	13:23	702P	EAST MID TWR	ONE ONE NINER SIX FIVE FOR SEVEN O TWO PAPA	P2	FLAPS ONE	NOISE OF LEVER MOVEMENT
		702P	EAST MID APP	EAST MIDLAND - EAST MIDLAND SEVEN ZERO TWO PAPA GOOD MORNING			
		EAST MID APP	702P	SEVEN ZERO TWO PAPA GOOD MORNING SQUAWK SEVEN THREE SIX FIVE IDENT MAINTAIN FLIGHT LEVEL FOUR ZERO ON REACHING			
		702P	EAST MID APP	EAST ROGER (TWO) THREE SIX FIVE IDENTING AND WE ARE MAINTAINING FOUR ZERO	P1	IT'S DONE	
		EAST MID APP	702P	ROGER	P1	AFTER TAKE OFF	
					P2	FLAPS UP	NOISE OF LEVER MOVEMENT
					P1	AFTER TAKE OFF AIR CONDITIONING AND PRESS SET START SWITCHES LOW ALTIMETERS AND INSTRUMENTS SET	

TIME GMT	TIME TO END	FROM	TO	RTF COMMUNICATION	ORIGIN	FLIGHT DECK COMMUNICATION	REMARKS
9:40					P1	LANDING GEAR UP AND OFF	
					P1	FLAPS UP NO LIGHTS LANDING LIGHTS OFF COMPLETE	
					P1	DESCENT AND APPROACH CHECK-LIST	
					P1	LOOSE OBJECTS SECURED	
					P1	APPROACH BRIEFING REVIEWED	
					P1	ANT-ICE ON	
					P1	AIR-CONDITIONING AND PRESS SET	
					P1	START SWITCHES LOW	
					P1	ALTIMETERS AND INSTRUMENTS	
	12:21	EAST MID APP	702P	SEVEN ZERO TWO PAPA CONTACT BIRMINGHAM ONE ONE EIGHT DECIMAL ZERO FIVE			
		702P	EAST MID APP	ONE ONE EIGHT ZERO FIVE BIRMINGHAM SEVEN ZERO TWO PAPA GOODBYE			
		EAST MID APP	702P	BYE			
		702P	BIRM	BIRMINGHAM GOOD MORNING SEVEN ZERO TWO PAPA FLIGHT LEVEL FOUR ZERO			
		BIRM	702P	ACE CARGO SEVEN ZERO TWO PAPA BIRMINGHAM SQUAWK FOUR SEVEN TWO THREE			
		702P	BIRM	FOUR SEVEN TWO THREE IS COMING			

TIME GMT	TIME TO END	FROM	TO	RTF COMMUNICATION	ORIGIN	FLIGHT DECK COMMUNICATION	REMARKS
9:41				OTHER ATC TRANSMISSIONS			
					?		
					?		
	11:09	BIRM	702P	ACE CARGO SEVEN ZERO TWO IS IDENTIFIED RADAR VECTORS RUNWAY TWO THREE AT COVENTRY			
		702P	BIRM	SEVEN ZERO TWO PAPA			
		BIRM	702P	SEVEN ZERO TWO PAPA CONTINUE TOWARDS THE CHARLIE TANGO AT FLIGHT LEVEL FOUR ZERO			
		702P	BIRM	ROGER WE ARE MAINTAINING FOUR ZERO SEVEN ZERO TWO PAPA			
				OTHER ATC TRANSMISSIONS			
					?		
					P1	*SET TWO THREE TWO*	
9:42				OTHER ATC TRANSMISSIONS			

TIME GMT	TIME TO END	FROM	TO	RTF COMMUNICATION	ORIGIN	FLIGHT DECK COMMUNICATION	REMARKS
					P2	*(? ONE THOUSAND)*	
					P1	*THE MET CONDITIONS ARE VERY BAD*	
					P1	*ASK FOR DESCENT*	
					P2	*GO AHEAD*	
	9:45	702P	BIRM	SEVEN ZERO TWO PAPA REQUESTING DESCENT			
9:43				OTHER ATC TRANSMISSIONS			
	9:31	BIRM	702P	ACE SEVEN ZERO TWO PAPA TURN LEFT HEADING ONE ONE ZERO			
		702P	BIRM	SEVEN ZERO TWO PAPA TURN LEFT HEADING ONE ONE ZERO			
		BIRM	702P	ACE SEVEN ZERO TWO PAPA DESCEND TO ALTITUDE TWO THOUSAND FIVE HUNDRED FEET BIRMINGHAM QNH ONE ZERO TWO TWO			
		702P	BIRM	SEVEN ZERO TWO PAPA DESCEND DOWN TWO THOUSAND FIVE HUNDRED FEET ON QNH ONE ZERO TWO TWO	P2	*(TWO)*	
				OTHER ATC TRANSMISSIONS			

TIME GMT	TIME TO END	FROM	TO	RTF COMMUNICATION	ORIGIN	FLIGHT DECK COMMUNICATION	REMARKS
				OTHER ATC TRANSMISSIONS			
	8:55	BIRM	702P	SEVEN ZERO TWO PAPA CONTACT COVENTRY ONE TWO TWO DECIMAL ZERO	P2	?	
	8:44			OTHER ATC TRANSMISSIONS	P2	SET ONE TWO TWO ZERO	ALTITUDE ALERT (3500FT)
9:44				OTHER ATC TRANSMISSIONS			
	8:29	702P	COV	CONTROL-ER ACE CARGO SEVEN ZERO TWO PAPA GOOD MORNING			
		COV	702P	SEVEN ZERO TWO PAPA GOOD MORNING IDENTIFIED ON HANDOVER FROM BIRMINGHAM RADAR WHAT'S YOUR PRESENT HEADING			(VOLUME ON SPEAKER INCREASED)
		702P	COV	NOW WE HAVE HEADING ER ONE ONE ZERO CROSSING THREE THOUSAND FEET DOWN TWENTY FIVE HUNDRED FEET QNH			
		COV	702P	ROGER THANK YOU VERY MUCH CONTINUE PRESENT HEADING FOR THE MOMENT IT WILL BE RADAR VECTORING FOR THE ILS APPROACH RUNWAY TWO THREE IDENTIFIED ON HANDOVER FROM BIRMINGHAM RADAR			

TIME GMT	TIME TO END	FROM	TO	RTF COMMUNICATION	ORIGIN	FLIGHT DECK COMMUNICATION	REMARKS
		702P	COV	THANK YOU	P2	WE CAN GO THROUGH	
					P1	WE GO	
					P2	(THIRTY HUNDRED)	
	7:51	COV	702P	ACE SEVEN ZERO TWO PAPA TURN LEFT NOW ONTO RADAR HEADING ZERO NINER ZERO	P1	WATCH THE SPEED	
	7:29	702P	COV	SEVEN ZERO TWO PAPA TURN LEFT HEADING ZERO NINER ZERO	P1	(FLAPS)	
9:45					P1	TAKE TWO HUNDRED AND TEN KNOTS	
					P2	TWO HUNDRED AND TEN	
	7:16	COV	702P	ACE CARGO SEVEN ZERO TWO PAPA SET QFE ONE ZERO ONE THREE DESCEND TO MAINTAIN HEIGHT ONE THOUSAND FIVE HUNDRED FEET AND TURN LEFT HEADING ZERO THREE ZERO			
		702P	COV	ACE CARGO SEVEN ZERO TWO PAPA WE TURN LEFT HEADING ZERO EIGHT ZERO AND WE DESCEND DOWN ONE FIVE ZERO ZERO FEET HEIGHT FOX ECHO ONE ZERO ONE THREE			
		COV	702P	ROGER THAT WAS -ER - ONTO RADAR HEADING NOW OF ZERO ONE ZERO PLEASE			

TIME GMT	TIME TO END	RTF COMMUNICATION			FLIGHT DECK COMMUNICATION		REMARKS
		FROM	TO		ORIGIN		
		702P	COV	ROGER TURN RIGHT TO ZERO ONE ZERO			
	6:44	COV	702P	SEVEN ZERO TWO PAPA WE'LL BE TAKING YOU THROUGH THE FINAL APPROACH TRACK FOR SPACING	P1	FLAPS	
					P2	ONE	
9:46		COV	702P	SEVEN ZERO TWO PAPA ARE YOU ABLE TO TAKE UP THE ILS AT COVENTRY NOW OR WOULD YOU LIKE AN SRA			
		702P	COV	AH SORRY CONFIRM YOUR MESSAGE PLEASE			
	6:30	COV	702P	ROGER COULD YOU TURN LEFT IMMEDIATELY NOW ONTO A HEADING OF ZERO ONE ZERO INITIALLY PLEASE			SOUND OF LEVER BUZZER
		702P	COV	WE HAVE PRESENTLY HEADING ZERO ONE ZERO			
		COV	702P	ROGER AT THE MOMENT YOU'RE TRACKING ONE ZERO ZERO CAN YOU TURN LEFT ZERO ONE ZERO PLEASE			

F-10

TIME GMT	TIME TO END	FROM	TO	RTF COMMUNICATION	ORIGIN	FLIGHT DECK COMMUNICATION	REMARKS
	6:15	702P	COV	ROGER	P2	ZERO ONE ZERO	
					P2	FLAPS FIVE	PITCH TRIM
					P1	*ZERO TEN THE HEADING*	
					P1	*HEADING TWO HUNDRED THIRTY*	
	5:54			**EXTRACT ENDS**	P1	*IF WE CONCENTRATE WE CAN GET IT*	NOISE OF ENGINE POWER INCREASE TO 70%
					P1	*THE PROBLEM IS NO ILS*	
	5:45			**EXTRACT BEGINS**	P2	FLAPS TEN	
	5:32	COV	702P	ACE CARGO SEVEN ZERO TWO PAPA CONTINUE THE LEFT TURN NOW ONTO RADAR HEADING OF TWO SIX ZERO			
9:47		702P	COV	ROGER WE TURN LEFT HEADING TWO SIX ZERO SEVEN ZERO TWO PAPA	P1	*IF WE CANT GET IT GO AROUND AND WE TRY AGAIN* *IF WE GIVE ATTENTION TO THE FUEL*	POWER REDUCED FROM 63% TO 53% POWER INCREASE TO 65%

TIME GMT	TIME TO END	FROM	TO	RTF COMMUNICATION	ORIGIN	FLIGHT DECK COMMUNICATION	REMARKS
9:48	4:40	COV	702P	AND SEVEN ZERO TWO PAPA APPROXIMATELY TWELVE NAUTICAL MILES NOW TO RUN FOR SURVEILLANCE RADAR APPROACH RUNWAY TWO THREE THAT APPROACH TERMINATES AT TWO NAUTICAL MILES FROM TOUCHDOWN CHECK YOUR MINIMA AND MISSED APPROACH POINT			
		702P	COV	ER - ROGER MADAM ER COULD YOU GIVE AAH COOPERATION WITH AH S R E -ER- APPROACH			
		COV	702P	ROGER A SURVEILLANCE RADAR APPROACH FOR RUNWAY TWO THREE			
		702P	COV	ROGER THANK YOU BECAUSE WE ARE NOT READING THE ILS			POWER REDUCTION 65% to 60%
	4:02	COV	702P	THAT'S ALL COPIED THANK YOU VERY MUCH YOU'RE TEN MILES FROM TOUCHDOWN NOW AT YOUR CONVENIENCE CHECK YOUR WHEELS YOU'RE CLOSING THE FINAL APPROACH TRACK VERY GENTLY FROM THE LEFT			INCREASED BACKGROUND NOISE

TIME GMT	TIME TO END	FROM	TO	RTF COMMUNICATION	ORIGIN	FLIGHT DECK COMMUNICATION	REMARKS
	3:53	702P	COV	OKAY WE ARE GEAR DOWN			
	3:50	COV	702P	THANK YOU			
					P2	FLAPS FIFTEEN	SOUND OF LEVER MOVEMENT INCREASED POWER TO 70 %
					P2	CHECK - THREE GREENS	
	3:55	702P	COV	DISTANCE TO FOR TOUCHDOWN AH - SEVEN ZERO TWO PAPA			
9:49	3:31	COV	702P	ROGER MILES FROM TOUCHDOWN NOW NINE TRACK MILES NINER TRACK MILES FROM TOUCHDOWN			
		702P	COV	ROGER			
		COV	702P	YOU CAN EXPECT FURTHER DESCENT TO MAINTAIN A THREE DEGREE GLIDEPATH AT FOUR AND A HALF MILES FROM TOUCHDOWN I'LL KEEP YOU ADVISED			
		702P	COV	OKAY THANK YOU VERY MUCH			

TIME GMT	TIME TO END	RTF COMMUNICATION			ORIGIN	FLIGHT DECK COMMUNICATION	REMARKS
		FROM	TO				
	3:11				P2	WE CAN SEE THE GROUND	
					P1	EH	
					P2	WE CAN SEE THE GROUND	
					P1	FROM TIME TO TIME	
					P1	IT'S NOT ALWAYS THE CASE	
					P2	IN PATCHES	
					P2	IT'S IN PATCHES	
					P1	OTHERWISE WE COME HERE AND TRY TO GET BELOW CLOUD	
	2:57	COV	702P	SEVEN ZERO TWO PAPA IS VERY SLIGHTLY LEFT OF TRACK CLOSING VERY GENTLY			
		702P	COV	ER - WOULD YOU WANT WE TURN RIGHT HEADING TWO SEVEN ZERO			
		COV	702P	NEGATIVE IF YOU CONTINUE ON THAT HEADING YOU WILL BE ON THE FINAL APPROACH TRACK BY SIX MILES			
		702P	COV	ROGER			
					P1	LOOK AT ADF ONE	

TIME GMT	TIME TO END	RTF COMMUNICATION			FLIGHT DECK COMMUNICATION		REMARKS
		FROM	TO		ORIGIN		
	2:34	COV	702P	SEVEN ZERO TWO PAPA TURN LEFT NOW TWO FOUR ZERO THE RADAR HEADING FINAL APPROACH TRACK			
9:50		702P	COV	ROGER SEVEN ZERO TWO PAPA TURN LEFT ON TWO FOUR ZERO			
				EXTRACT ENDS			ENGINE 62%-64% PITCH TRIM
				EXTRACT BEGINS	P1	*TURN TURN TURN TWO HUNDRED AND FORTY*	
	2:11	COV	702P	TURN FURTHER LEFT NOW TWO THREE ZERO THE HEADING TWO THREE ZERO			
		702P	COV	TURN LEFT TWO THREE ZERO			
					P1	*QUICKLY*	SOUND OF POWER INCREASE TO 74%
					P1	*ONE HUNDRED AND FIFTY*	
	1:55				P1	*PUT ON FIVE DEGREES MORE TO THE LEFT*	
	1:52	COV	702P	AND YOU'RE SIX MILES FROM TOUCHDOWN NOW QFE CHECK ONE ZERO ZERO ONE THREE NICELY ON THE FINAL APPROACH TRACK THE HEADING GOOD			

TIME GMT	TIME TO END	FROM	TO	RTF COMMUNICATION	FLIGHT DECK COMMUNICATION ORIGIN	REMARKS
		702P	COV	ROGER		CLICKING PITCH TRIM
		COV	702P	FIVE AND A HALF MILES FROM TOUCHDOWN TWO THREE ZERO THE HEADING ON TRACK		POWER REDUCTION 72% - 67%
	1:44	COV	702P	TURN RIGHT FIVE DEGREES TWO THREE FIVE FIVE FROM TOUCHDOWN TWO THREE FIVE IS THE HEADING COMMENCE DESCENT NOW TO MAINTAIN A THREE DEGREE GLIDEPATH, YOU SHOULD BE LEAVING HEIGHT ONE THOUSAND FIVE HUNDRED FEET		
	1:28			TWO THREE FIVE IS THE RADAR HEADING ON TRACK FOUR AND A HALF MILES FROM TOUCHDOWN HEIGHT ONE FOUR ZERO ZERO FEET TWO THREE FIVE THE RADAR HEADING TURN		(POSSIBLE MOVEMENT OF FLAP)
	1:21			FURTHER RIGHT RADAR HEADING TWO FOUR ZERO FOUR MILES FROM TOUCHDOWN YOUR HEIGHT SHOULD BE ONE TWO FIVE ZERO FEET TWO FOUR ZERO THE HEADING		
9:51	1:09			THREE AND A HALF MILES FROM TOUCHDOWN YOUR HEIGHT SHOULD BE ONE THOUSAND ONE HUNDRED FEET		MULTIPLE CLICKING
	1:01			TWO FOUR ZERO THE RADAR HEADING VERY VERY SLIGHTLY LEFT OF TRACK AND CLOSING GENTLY TWO FOUR ZERO THE HEADING		

TIME GMT	TIME TO END	FROM	TO	RTF COMMUNICATION	ORIGIN	FLIGHT DECK COMMUNICATION	REMARKS
	0:48	COV	702P	THREE MILES FROM TOUCHDOWN YOUR HEIGHT SHOULD BE NINE FIVE ZERO FEET ON TRACK TURN LEFT HEADING TWO THREE EIGHT TWO THREE EIGHT THE			PITCH TRIM
				HEADING TWO AND A HALF MILES FROM TOUCHDOWN YOUR HEIGHT SHOULD BE EIGHT ZERO ZERO FEET			POWER INCREASE
	0:26			TWO THREE EIGHT YOU'RE CLEARED TO LAND RUNWAY TWO THREE THE SURFACE WIND VARIABLE LESS THAN FIVE KNOTS			PITCH TRIM
9:52	0:23			TWO MILES FROM TOUCHDOWN YOUR HEIGHT SHOULD BE SIX FIVE ZERO FEET CHECK MINIMUM DESCENT HEIGHT ON TRACK THE HEADING GOOD TWO THREE EIGHT THE RADAR HEADING YOU ARE CLEAR TO LAND TURN FURTHER RIGHT TWO FOUR ZERO DRIFTING VERY SLIGHTLY LEFT OF TRACK TWO FOUR ZERO TWO FOUR ZERO IS THE RADAR HEADING NICELY ON TRACK NOW			
	0:01			THE HEADING IS GOOD		EXCLAMATION	
	0						END OF RECORDING

F-17

AN ANALYSIS OF THE IMPACT BETWEEN THE AIRCRAFT AND THE TOWER, AND SUBSEQUENT FLIGHT PATH

Tower construction

The electricity tower comprised a lattice girder structure 26.4 metres high supporting six 132 kV high tension phase conductor cables arranged in two sets of three, one set on each side of the tower, together with a single earth cable carried at the apex of the tower, see Figure 1. Each cable was suspended from its support arm by a stack of interlocking ceramic insulators approximately 2 metres in length. Vibration dampers, each comprising a pair of weights attached to arms, were clamped to each conductor cable a short distance from their attachment to the insulators.

The high tension cables each comprised a multi-stranded steel core of approximately 8 mm diameter overlaid with a multi-stranded outer layer of aluminium wire, increasing the outer diameter to 20 mm. The multi-strand earth cable was of steel only, and was 13 mm in diameter.

The tower impact

The aircraft struck the tower at a position approximately level with the mid set of support arms, severing the tower structure at this level and causing the upper section of tower to topple to the ground. The lower pair of support arms and their attached cables were intact and essentially undamaged. The mid set of support arms and the intervening tower structure was totally disrupted by the aircraft impact but the mid set of cables survived relatively intact, evidently because they had become unhooked during the impact process, and were hanging down on each side of the tower suspended between the two adjoining towers. The aluminium outer strands of the mid-conductor cable on the aircraft down-track side of the tower had been torn and dragged along the length of the cable as a result of attachment clamps being dragged along the cable during the impact process, but no evidence of contact with the aircraft was apparent on either of the mid-cables.

Both of the top conductor cables and the earth cable were broken, and were found on the ground having recoiled out to either side of the tower. (These cables had been cut and partially removed from site by the electricity company in the immediate aftermath of the accident, prior to AAIB arrival on site.) Of these two cables, that on the aircraft's approach side had failed at a position approximately 10.5 metres to the right of the suspension point (viewed from the aircraft's approach direction) due to tension overload of the steel core. The aluminium outer strands of this cable were extensively bunched, due to the outer strands being forced along the inner core, away from the tower, during the impact process. The corresponding cable on the down-track side of the tower had failed in a similar manner at a point approximately 7 metres from the tower.

The earth line had failed in tension overload at a position similar to that of the two upper conductor cables.

It was not possible to identify positively any evidence of splash caused by arcing contact between a conductor and the aircraft structure.

Wreckage distribution

Debris from both the tower and aircraft was distributed on the ground along the aircraft's flight path between the initial impact with the electricity tower and the final ground impact in the woods bordering the southern edge of the housing estate. Figure 2 is a sketch plan showing the general distribution of wreckage, together with relevant ground features.

The greater part of this debris was found in the fields immediately forward of the pylon impact, and comprised:

- the upper part of the tower structure, with upper conductor support arms still attached (though deformed)

- the twisted remains of the mid-conductor support arms

- numerous miscellaneous lengths of heavily deformed angle iron from the tower structure

- lengths of phase conductor and earth cable

- fragments of, and clusters of intact, ceramic insulator blocks

- small pieces of leading edge flap and wing leading structure from the mid region of the left wing

- the whole of the left wing trailing edge mid-section fore flap, in four pieces

- sections of left engine fan cowling

- the left engine slipper fairing (between the fan cowl and leading edge)

- left wing boat (flap track) fairings

- both nose landing gear doors, complete

- large quantities of unidentified wing leading edge, miscellaneous fibreglass and honeycomb fragments, and general structural debris

Wreckage was less densely distributed in the areas beyond the field, the principal items comprising:

- the left wingtip and outermost 2 metres of left wing, which was lodged in a tree in the garden of No 16 Fieldmarch; adjacent to the end of wall of the house, which was damaged

- miscellaneous sections of heavily deformed angle iron from the tower structure, including one piece with brick dust adhering, found in the road adjacent to No 17 Fieldmarch (the chimney of which was damaged), and at the final impact site

- pieces of left aileron and left outboard leading edge flap, also found in the road adjacent to No 17 Fieldmarch

- miscellaneous metal, fibreglass, and honeycomb fragments

The remaining aircraft wreckage was contained within the main ground impact zone, which began at a point just beyond the edge of the road bounding the southeast corner of the housing estate.

Evidence from initial impact with tower

The wreckage from both the tower structure and the aircraft were examined in detail for evidence associated with the initial stages of the tower impact, with a view to facilitating subsequent correlation between the aircraft and tower damage patterns aimed at establishing the aircraft's attitude and flight path at the instant of tower contact.

The following evidence was noted on the tower wreckage (see Figure 3):

- A red paint smear on the outer surface of the main (corner) upright of the tower, on the approach side of the tower and on the right side (viewed along track). The smear extended over a distance of approximately 200 mm and was centred approximately 1 metre below the mid-conductor support arm.

- Severe buckling and associated localised heavy indentations of the angle iron components forming the outer end of the lower spanwise member of the mid-support arm on the approach side of the tower. This localised damage comprised regularly spaced notches in the free (outer) edge of the horizontal flange of this member over a 550 mm spanwise length of the arm beginning at a position approximately 1 metre from the end of the arm; sooting of the vertical flange was also apparent over this same spanwise region.

- Two distinct contact bruises were also evident on the vertical flange of this member at positions approximately 335 mm and 425 mm (toward the tower) from the region of indentation-damage and sooting. These two bruises were approximately parallel to one another, and were inclined slightly from the vertical.

- A small fragment of fibreglass honeycomb sandwich structure was embedded between plates at the free end of the mid-conductor support arm on the down-track side of the tower.

- A second small fragment of similar honeycomb material was embedded in the joint plate at the junction between the bottom rail of the mid-conductor support arm on the approach side of the tower and the left side main upright (viewed along the approach).

The following evidence was noted on the left engine wreckage (see Figure 4):

- A series of deep chordwise cuts into the left engine compressor stator blades was found. These cuts were all in the same plane and had evidently been produced simultaneously. The cuts displayed highly serrated fracture faces consistent with high speed tearing, such as would occur if stator had been driven into the free edge of one of the flanges of the angle-iron tower elements. The orientation of the plane of these cuts, in terms of both longitudinal (pitch) and lateral (roll) angles in relation to the engine axes is illustrated in Figure 4 (the blue coloured blade is at engine bottom centre).

- Several broader regions of leading edge bruising were also apparent on several of the stator blades at locations just above the cuts. Each bruise was of similar form and width (typically 65 mm), and had evidently been caused by contact with the flat side of one or more of the angle-iron elements of the tower structure. The thick magenta lines in Figure 4 indicate the positions of these bruises.

The following evidence was noted on the aircraft wreckage:

- Front-to-rear crush damage to the left outboard side engine fan cowl, caused by a heavy grazing impact, in the vicinity of a red painted line which runs circumferentially around the cowl. A comparative chemical analysis of the red smear film from the tower and a sample of the red paint from the engine cowl produced excellent correlation between the samples, indicating beyond reasonable doubt that the paint smear on the tower was caused by contact with the left engine cowl.

- A longitudinal cable-cut into the left-hand nose gear door, running aft into the door from its forward edge a distance of 690 mm. The plane of the cable-cut was approximately at right angles to the plane of the door, and the cut-line was angled downwards slightly in relation to the bottom edge of the door (door at gear extended position), approximately parallel with the fuselage belly-profile. The (conductor) cable was firmly embedded in the door structure at the end of the cut, and the outer strands of the cable had been bunched up in a manner consistent with the door having slid along the steel core of the cable from left to right (relative to aircraft track) as the cable had sliced back into the door.

- No corresponding cable-cut was present on the right-hand nose gear door; instead, a light chamfer had been ground onto the upper top edge over the forward part of the door, consistent with a cable having slid along the in the gap between the door and the belly of aircraft. The hinges of this door were broken in a manner consistent with this scenario.

A survey of the honeycomb materials used on the engine cowl and wing structure suggested that each of the two fragments of honeycomb material found embedded in the joint plates of the tower, described earlier, originated from the flap track boat-fairings.

Analysis

Impact parameters

The weight, bulk, and highly deformed nature of the tower wreckage precluded a physical reconstruction of the aircraft and tower wreckage, in the conventional manner, to facilitate correlation of impact witness marks. Instead, three-dimensional computer models were constructed of the upper part of the tower and the aircraft, the latter comprising the external form of the aircraft overall with more detailed modelling of the landing gear door and engine stator assembly. The correlation between damage marks on both tower and aircraft components, caused during the initial stages of the tower collision and detailed in the preceding section, was then explored by adjusting the relative position of the computer model of the aircraft in relation to that of the tower until a reasonable match was achieved.

A similar approach was adopted in relation to the wingtip collision with the house at No 16 Fieldmarch, and the passage of the aircraft through the lighting pole and trees during the initial stages of the ground impact.

Tower impact parameters

Figure 5 shows the best fit achieved between the aircraft/engine and the tower computer models. With the aircraft positioned in this attitude, the position of the left engine stator damage matches almost exactly with the region of heavy localised damage and sooting on the mid-conductor support arm on the approach side of the tower. Furthermore:

- the orientation of the plane of the stator blade-cuts matches the orientation of the horizontal flange of the arm's lower member,

- the flatter bruises on the blades are broadly consistent with the positions of the vertical flanges of the spanwise and bracing elements of the arm, and

- the two bruises on the vertical flange of the arm member coincide almost exactly with the position of the outboard sector of the intake casing.

With the engine in this position, the red paint smear on the tower matches the position of the red paint line on the engine cowl. The lateral positions of the two fragments of fibreglass honeycomb material also match reasonably well with the two flap track fairings from which this material almost certainly originated, the slight lateral mis-match as-drawn being reduced in practice by rotation of the tower due to the initial impact of the engine into the support arm. The slight vertical mis-match implies that the aircraft was on a slightly climbing trajectory (bearing in mind that the relevant parts of the aircraft as-drawn still have some distance to travel before they meet their respective contact points on the tower structure).

Figures 6 and 7 illustrate the complete aircraft and tower interaction at the stage in the impact process when the red paint line on the cowl was contacting the tower upright. It can be seen that the upper phase conductor cable on the approach side of the tower would have passed just below the nose and run down under the belly of the aircraft until it met the landing gear doors.

At this point, due to the slight bank angle to the left, it would have entered the gap between the left nose gear door and the fuselage skin, and on the right side cut into the leading edge of the right-hand nose gear door. Thereafter, it would have sliced rearwards through the right-hand door, following the belly curvature of the aircraft and broken through the hinges of the left-hand door until it came up against the landing gear proper, at which point it would have broken due to tension overload.

Flight path following the tower impact

Figure 10 shows the estimated trajectory and aircraft attitudes following the tower impact. The aircraft height and attitude shown at the instant of the tower impact is that derived in the above analysis. The attitude and position of the aircraft at the instant of contact with the house at No 16 Fieldmarch was derived from matching of scrape and impact damage features on the left wingtip and on the gable end of the house. The attitude immediately prior to ground impact was determined from a study of aircraft geometry in relation to the heights at which trees and the lighting pole were severed. It should be noted that the ground rises slightly between the tower and the houses, before falling way again slightly toward the final impact site. The intermediate aircraft positions are estimates only.

Figure 10 shows that the aircraft evidently followed a slightly lofting flight path following impact with the tower, rolling violently to left but with the nose well above the horizon until after the impact with the house. The corresponding plan-view diagram in Figure 9 shows that the aircraft followed a curving flight path to the left of track.

The rapid roll to the left following the impact with the tower was undoubtedly caused by loss of left from the left wing following impact disruption of the leading and trailing edge flaps.

Figure 11 is a perspective view of those shown in Figures 9 and 10, showing the aircraft in relation to the housing estate over which it passed.

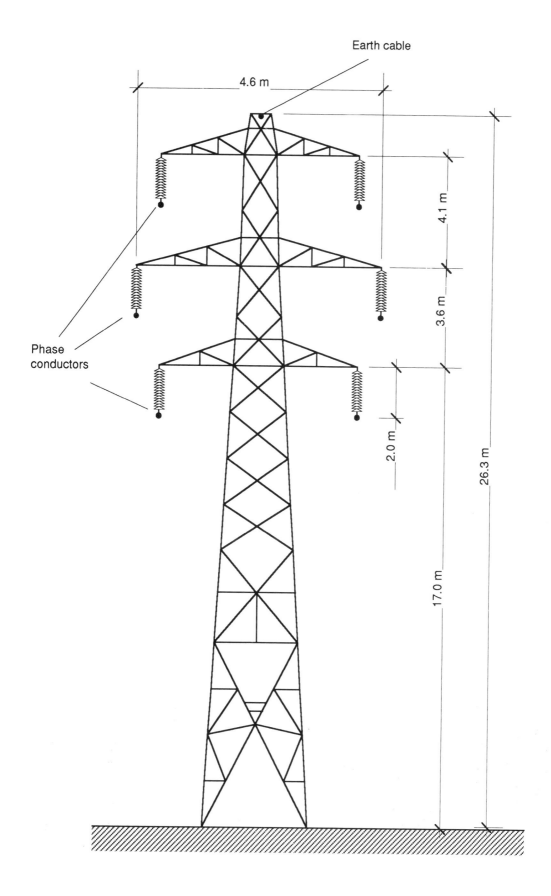

Earth cable

4.6 m

4.1 m

3.6 m

2.0 m

26.3 m

17.0 m

Phase
conductors

Figure 1

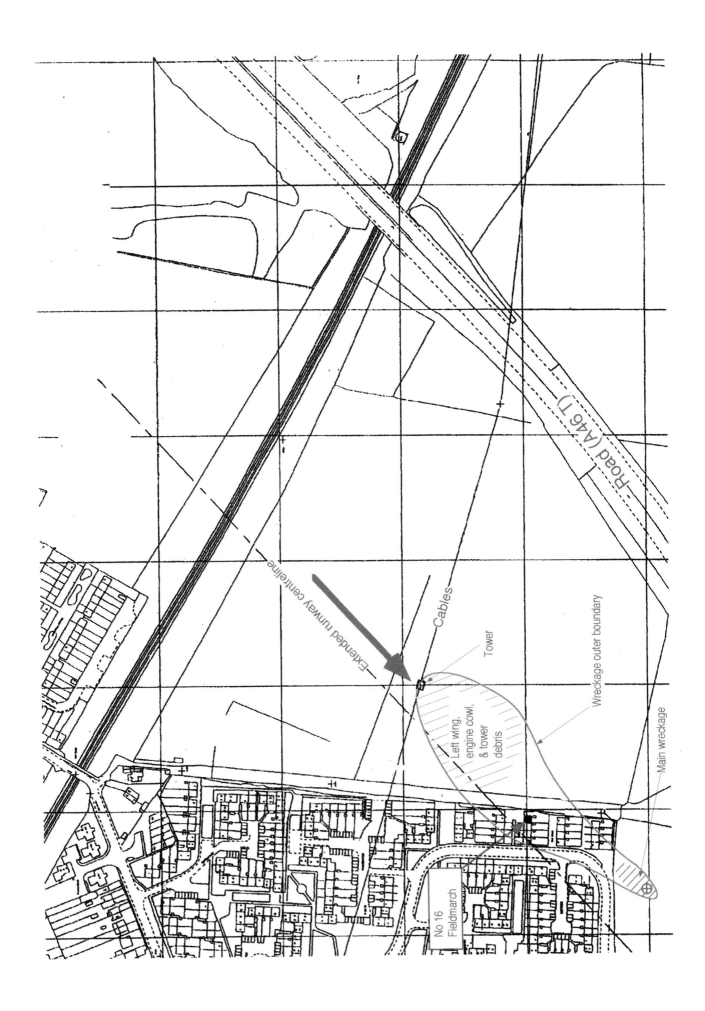

Figure 2

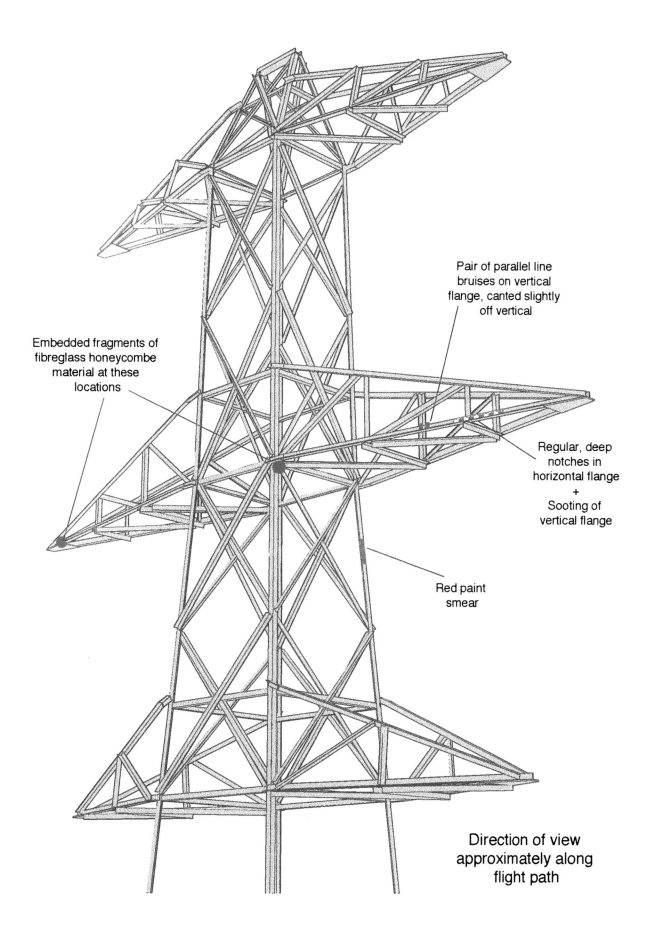

Pair of parallel line
bruises on vertical
flange, canted slightly
off vertical

Embedded fragments of
fibreglass honeycombe
material at these
locations

Regular, deep
notches in
horizontal flange
+
Sooting of
vertical flange

Red paint
smear

Direction of view
approximately along
flight path

Figure 3

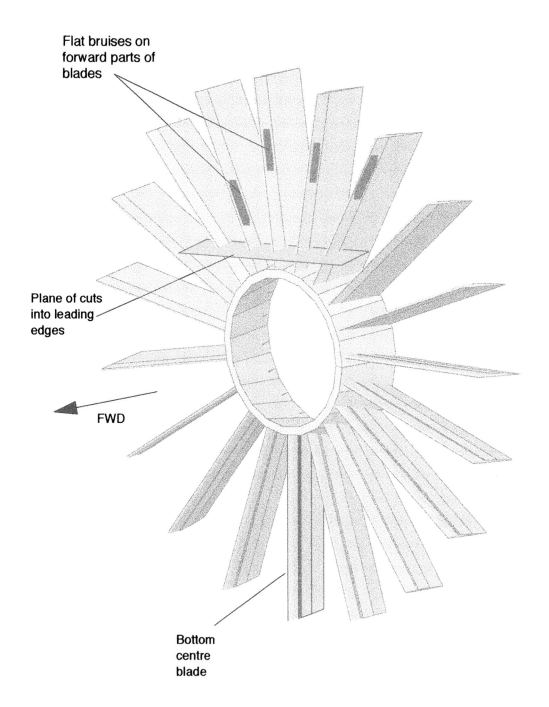

Flat bruises on
forward parts of
blades

Plane of cuts
into leading
edges

FWD

Bottom
centre
blade

Figure 4

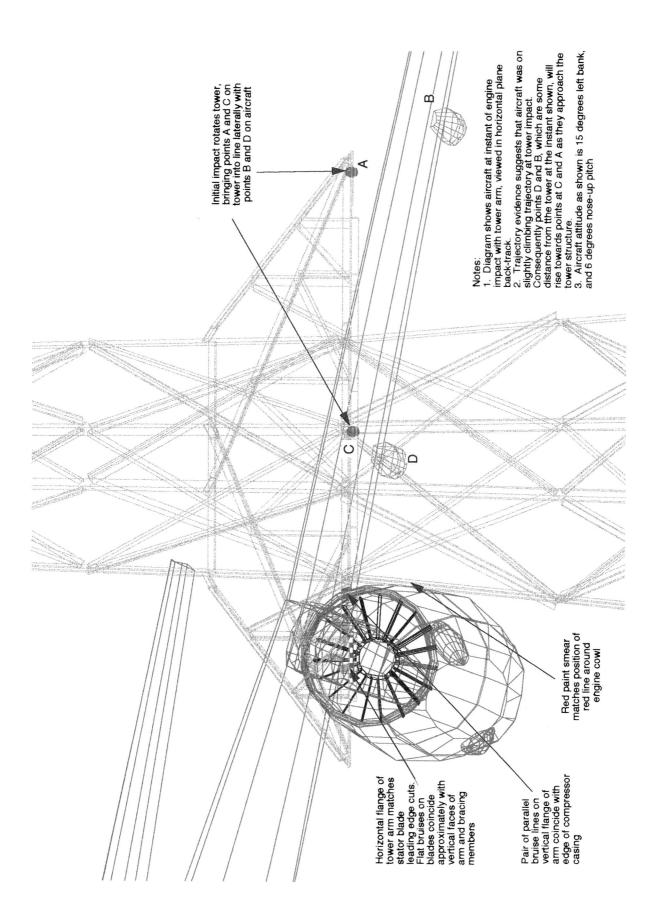

Initial impact rotates tower, bringing points A and C on tower into line laterally with points B and D on aircraft

A

B

C

D

Notes:
1. Diagram shows aircraft at instant of engine impact with tower arm, viewed in horizontal plane back-track.
2. Trajectory evidence suggests that aircraft was on slightly climbing trajectory at tower impact. Consequently points D and B, which are some distance from the tower at the instant shown, will rise towards points at C and A as they approach the tower structure.
3. Aircraft attitude as shown is 15 degrees left bank, and 6 degrees nose-up pitch

Red paint smear matches position of red line around engine cowl

Horizontal flange of tower arm matches stator blade leading edge cuts. Flat bruises on blades coincide approximately with vertical faces of arm and bracing members

Pair of parallel bruise lines on vertical flange of arm coincide with edge of compressor casing

Figure 5

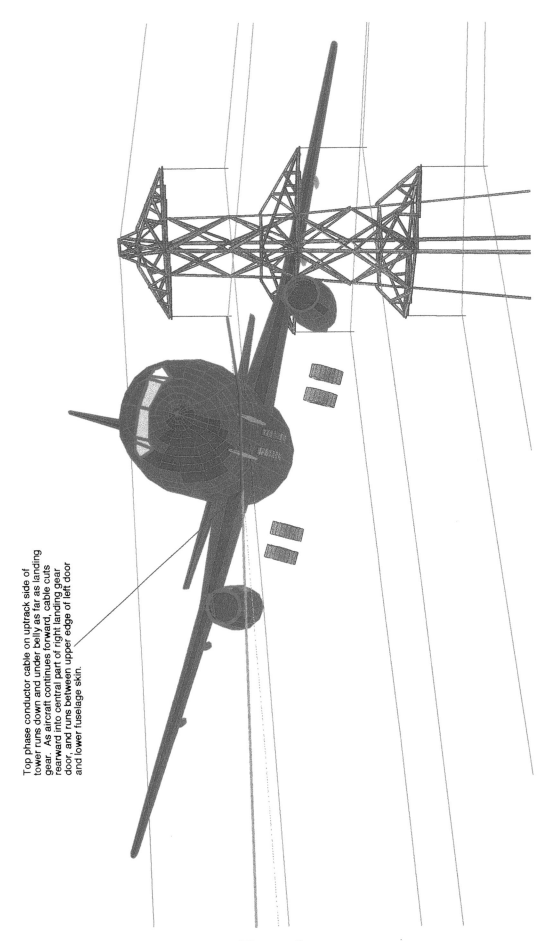

Top phase conductor cable on uptrack side of tower runs down and under belly as far as landing gear. As aircraft continues forward, cable cuts rearward into central part of right landing gear door, and runs between upper edge of left door and lower fuselage skin.

Figure 6

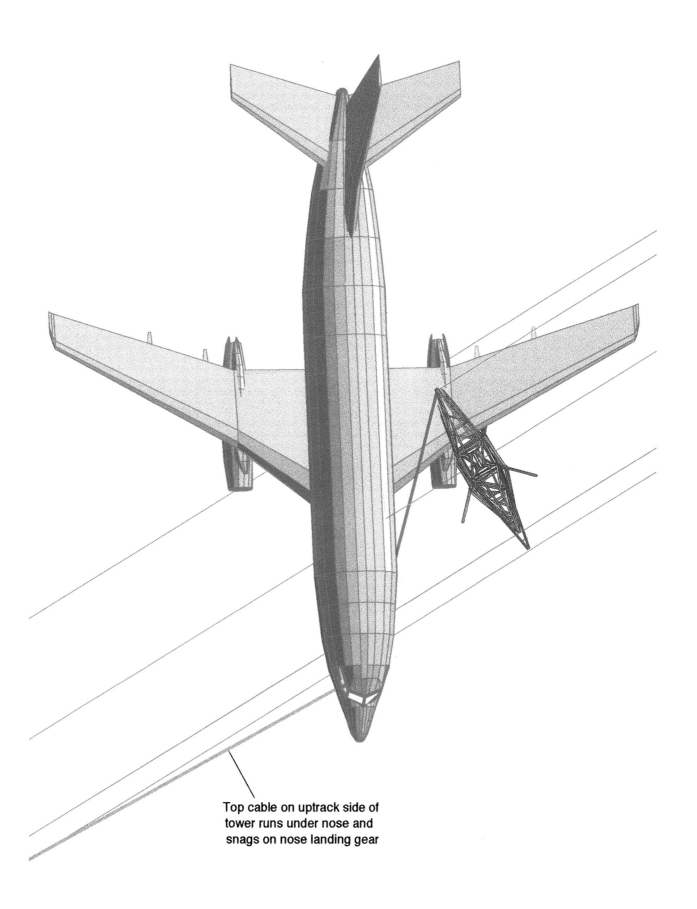

Top cable on uptrack side of tower runs under nose and snags on nose landing gear

Figure 7

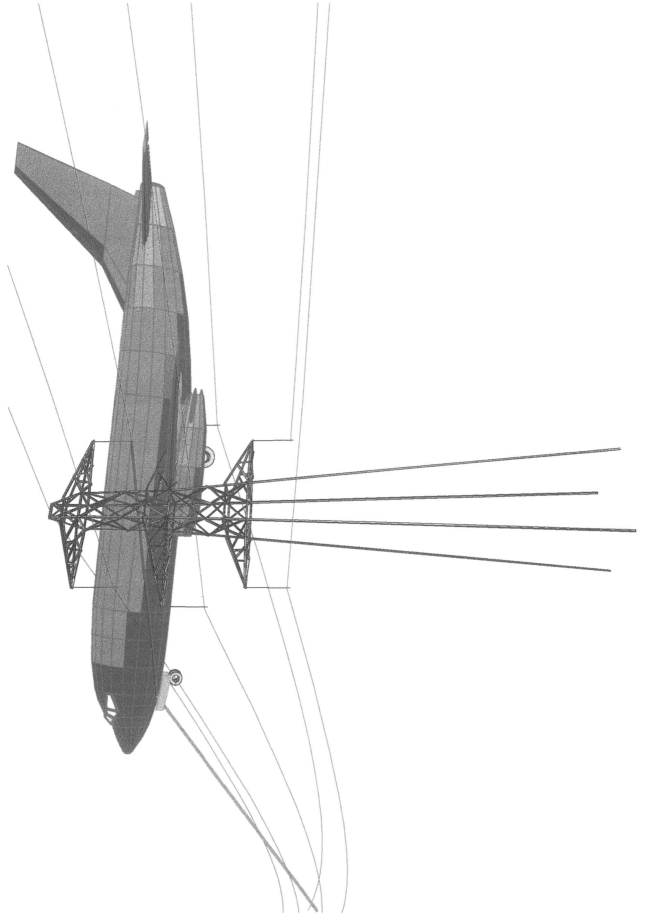

Figure 8

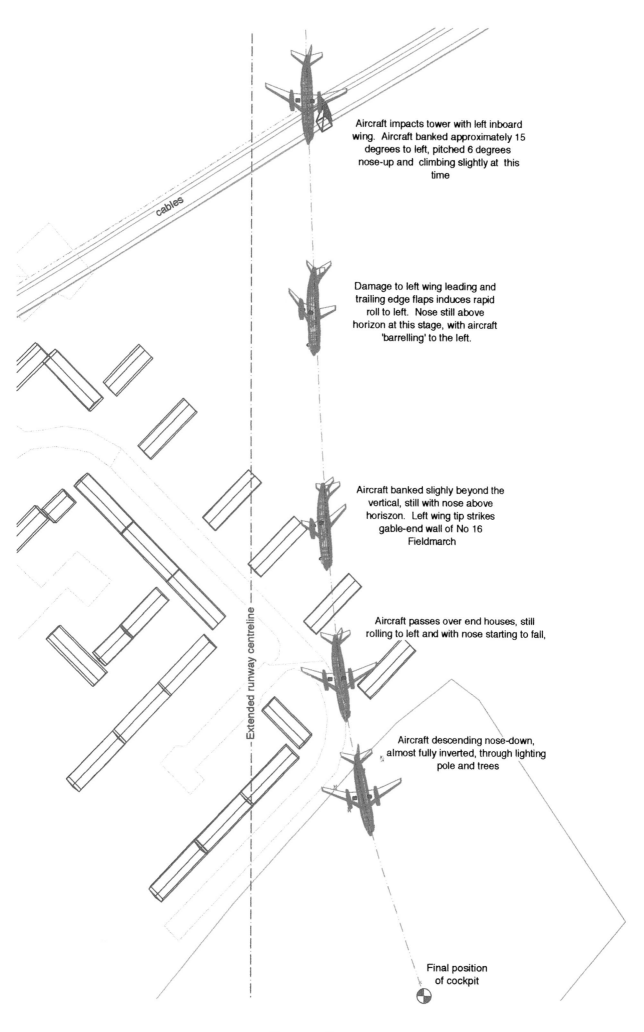

Aircraft impacts tower with left inboard wing. Aircraft banked approximately 15 degrees to left, pitched 6 degrees nose-up and climbing slightly at this time

Damage to left wing leading and trailing edge flaps induces rapid roll to left. Nose still above horizon at this stage, with aircraft 'barrelling' to the left.

Aircraft banked slighly beyond the vertical, still with nose above horiszon. Left wing tip strikes gable-end wall of No 16 Fieldmarch

Aircraft passes over end houses, still rolling to left and with nose starting to fall,

Aircraft descending nose-down, almost fully inverted, through lighting pole and trees

Final position of cockpit

cables

Extended runway centreline

Figure 9

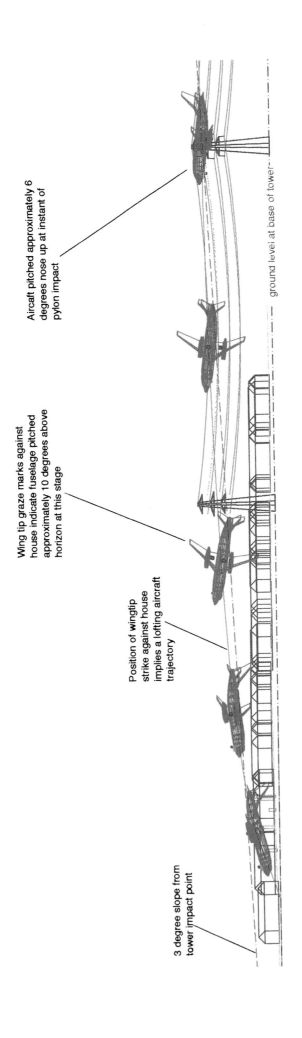

Aircaft pitched approximately 6 degrees nose up at instant of pylon impact

Wing tip graze marks against house indicate fuselage pitched approximately 10 degrees above horizon at this stage

Position of wingtip strike against house implies a lofting aircraft trajectory

3 degree slope from tower impact point

ground level at base of tower

Figure 10

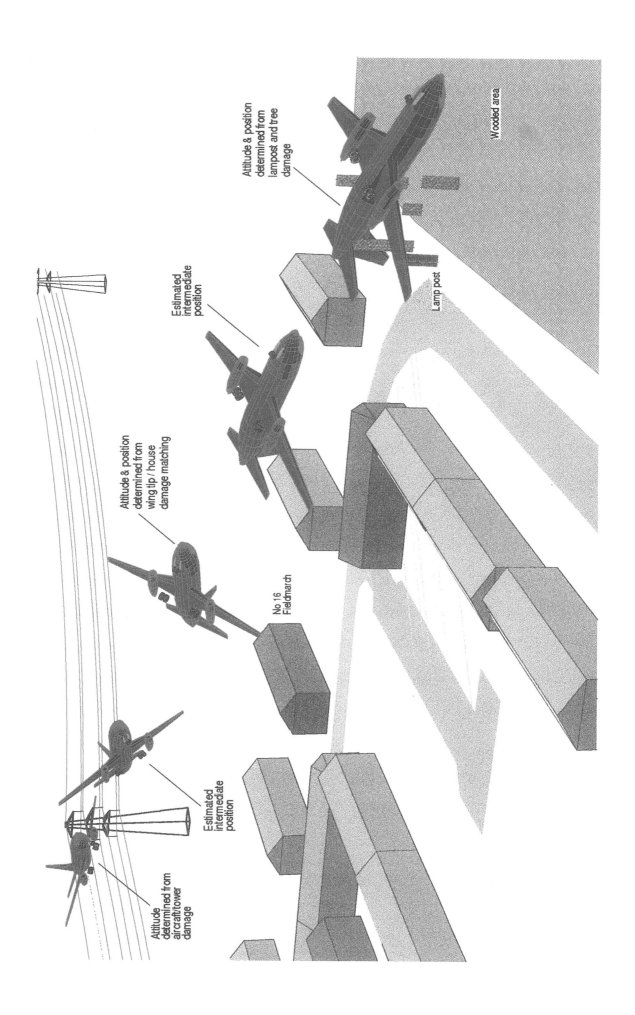

Figure 11

Coventry Runway 23 Approach - Range approx. 2 miles

VIEW OF APPROACH AREA FROM NORMAL GLIDEPATH

VIEW OF APPROACH AREA FROM LOW GLIDEPATH

7T-VEE FLIGHT OPERATIONS

OPERATIONS FROM/TO BOURNEMOUTH AIRPORT

DATE	DAY	DEP TIME	DEPART TO/ARRIVE FROM	ARR TIME
20-Oct	Thu	=	DAAG	1125
20-Oct	Thu	1641	EHAM	2111
21-Oct	Fri	1624	EHAM	2059
25-Oct	Tue	1552	EHAM	1938
26-Oct	Wed	0930	EHAM	1303
26-Oct	Wed	1451	EHAM	1803
26-Oct	Wed	1942	EHAM	2233
27-Oct	Thu	1331	EHAM	1619
27-Oct	Thu	1804	EHAM	2052
28-Oct	Fri	1305	EHAM	1537
29-Oct	Sat	0719	EGPK/LIMC	1714
29-Oct	Sat	1901	EHAM	2201
30-Oct	Sun	0741	DAAG	=
31-Oct	Mon	=	DAAG	0904
1-Nov	Tue	1250	EHAM	1548
1-Nov	Tue	1726	EHAM	2015
2-Nov	Wed	0805	EHAM	1128
2-Nov	Wed	1900	EHAM	=

OPERATIONS FROM/TO COVENTRY AIRPORT

DATE	DAY	DEP TIME	DEPART TO/ARRIVE FROM	ARR TIME
2-Nov	Wed	=	EHAM	2232
5-Nov	Sat	1044	EHAM	1332
5-Nov	Sat	1543	EHAM	1810
5-Nov	Sat	1955	EHAM	=
6-Nov	Sun	=	EHAM	0944
10-Nov	Thu	0519	EGLL	=
14-Nov	Mon	=	DAAG	1700
14-Nov	Mon	1756	LFRN/LFRU	2126
15-Nov	Tue	0930	EHAM	1219
15-Nov	Tue	1357	EHAM	1637
16-Nov	Wed	0950	LFRS	1347
16-Nov	Wed	1614	LFRS	2022
17-Nov	Thu	0730	LFRS	1048
17-Nov	Thu	1251	LFRS	1610
17-Nov	Thu	1837	LFRN	2123
18-Nov	Fri	0741	LFRN	1226
18-Nov	Fri	1359	LFRS	1723
18-Nov	Fri	1930	LFRN	2221
19-Nov	Sat	0500	EHAM	0748
19-Nov	Sat	0938	LFRN	1241
21-Nov	Mon	1038	LFRS	1337
21-Nov	Mon	1634	EHAM	1926
22-Nov	Tue	1022	LFRS	1316
22-Nov	Tue	1342	LFRS/LFRN	1842
23-Nov	Wed	1119	LFRN	1505
23-Nov	Wed	1644	LFRN	1957
23-Nov	Wed	2121	LFRN	=
24-Nov	Thu	=	LFRN	0036
24-Nov	Thu	0747	LFRN	1046
24-Nov	Thu	1101	LFRN	1438
24-Nov	Thu	1634	LFRN	1926
24-Nov	Thu	2103	LFRN	=
25-Nov	Fri	=	LFRN	0001

7T-VEE FLIGHT OPERATIONS

DATE	DAY	DEP TIME	DEPART TO/ARRIVE FROM	ARR TIME
25-Nov	Fri	0647	EHAM	0942
25-Nov	Fri	1024	LFRN	1413
25-Nov	Fri	1456	LFRN	1846
25-Nov	Fri	2009	LFRN	2325
26-Nov	Sat	0032	LFRN	0322
26-Nov	Sat	0439	EHAM	0658
26-Nov	Sat	0819	LFRN	1101
26-Nov	Sat	1341	EGLL	=
28-Nov	Mon	=	DAAG	0934
30-Nov	Wed	0807	EHAM	1143
30-Nov	Wed	1315	EHAM	1623
30-Nov	Wed	1829	LFRN	2142
1-Dec	Thu	0847	LFPO/LFRS	1727
1-Dec	Thu	1828	EHAM	2114
2-Dec	Fri	0031	EHAM	1212
2-Dec	Fri	1318	EHAM	1557
2-Dec	Fri	1724	EHAM	2043
3-Dec	Sat	0501	LFRN	0806
3-Dec	Sat	0953	EHAM	1305
3-Dec	Sat	1350	EGLL	=
4-Dec	Sun	=	DAAG	1859
5-Dec	Mon	0837	LFRN	1116
5-Dec	Mon	1238	LFRN	1528
5-Dec	Mon	1719	EHAM	2014
5-Dec	Mon	2119	LFRN	=
6-Dec	Tue	=	LFRN	0002
6-Dec	Tue	0511	LFRN	0813
6-Dec	Tue	0931	LFRN	1210
6-Dec	Tue	1332	EHAM	1642
6-Dec	Tue	1743	EHAM	2111
7-Dec	Wed	0250	LFRN	0438
7-Dec	Wed	0911	LFRN	1224
7-Dec	Wed	1417	EHAM	1722
7-Dec	Wed	1903	EHAM	2311
8-Dec	Thu	0104	EHAM	0359
8-Dec	Thu	0817	EHAM	1147
8-Dec	Thu	1522	LFRN	1827
8-Dec	Thu	2011	LFRN	=
9-Dec	Fri	=	LFRN	0010
9-Dec	Fri	0127	EHAM	0429
9-Dec	Fri	0548	LFRN	0938
9-Dec	Fri	1051	LFRN	1349
9-Dec	Fri	1511	LFRN	1734
9-Dec	Fri	1830	LFRN	2119
10-Dec	Sat	0303	EHAM	0546
10-Dec	Sat	0702	EHAM	0954
10-Dec	Sat	1206	EHAM	1456
10-Dec	Sat	1552	LFRN	1833
10-Dec	Sat	1941	EHAM	=
12-Dec	Mon	=	EHAM	0730
12-Dec	Mon	0928	LFRN	1219
12-Dec	Mon	1354	LFRN	1651
12-Dec	Mon	1751	EHAM	2043
13-Dec	Tue	0032	EHAM	0435
13-Dec	Tue	0555	EHAM	0853
13-Dec	Tue	0936	LFRN	1229
13-Dec	Tue	1328	LFRN	1611
13-Dec	Tue	1724	LFRN	2020

7T-VEE FLIGHT OPERATIONS

DATE	DAY	DEP TIME	DEPART TO/ARRIVE FROM	ARR TIME
14-Dec	Wed	0215	EHAM	0513
14-Dec	Wed	0627	EHAM	0954
14-Dec	Wed	1026	EHAM	1312
14-Dec	Wed	1412	LFRN	1645
14-Dec	Wed	1809	EHAM	2056
15-Dec	Thu	0137	EHAM	0415
15-Dec	Thu	0546	EHAM	0846
15-Dec	Thu	0952	LFRN	1258
15-Dec	Thu	1422	EHAM	1807
15-Dec	Thu	1926	LFRN	2231
16-Dec	Fri	0119	EHAM	0428
16-Dec	Fri	0622	LFRN	0857
16-Dec	Fri	0953	LFRN	1224
16-Dec	Fri	1329	LFRN	1618
16-Dec	Fri	1805	EHAM	2038
16-Dec	Fri	2205	EHAM	=
17-Dec	Sat	=	EHAM	0029
17-Dec	Sat	0207	EHAM	0448
17-Dec	Sat	0606	EHAM	0837
17-Dec	Sat	0956	LFRN	1225
17-Dec	Sat	1357	LFRN	1619
17-Dec	Sat	1730	EHAM	=
18-Dec	Sun	=	EHAM	1009
18-Dec	Sun	1328	DAAG	=
19-Dec	Mon	=	DAAG	1218
19-Dec	Mon	1325	LFRN	1602
19-Dec	Mon	1729	LFRN	1958
20-Dec	Tue	0116	EHAM	0355
20-Dec	Tue	0517	EHAM	0833
20-Dec	Tue	0930	EHAM	1206
20-Dec	Tue	1323	EHAM	1559
20-Dec	Tue	1727	LFRN	2014
21-Dec	Wed	0059	EHAM	0342
21-Dec	Wed	0452	EHAM	0735

KEY

CODE	AIRPORT
DAAG	ALGIERS
EHAM	AMSTERDAM
EGLL	LONDON HEATHROW
EGPK	PRESTWICK
LIMC	MILAN
LFRN	RENNES
LFRS	NANTES
LFPO	PARIS - ORLY
LFRU	MORLAIX

Public Safety Zones

Public Safety Zones (PSZs) were first introduced in 1958. They are established by the Department of Transport (DOT) at specified major airports in order to prevent any build-up of population in areas where there is a greater risk of an aircraft accident. The CAA acting on behalf of the DOT generally advises against the grant of planning permission for developments which are likely to increase significantly the numbers of persons residing, working or congregating in these zones. The advice given is formulated in accordance with policy directions from the DOT. Zones are included in the uncoloured areas in official safeguarding maps for aerodromes where PSZs are established. Aerodrome owners concerned and appropriate local authorities have been notified by the DOT of the grid reference co-ordinates defining each PSZ, which broadly coincides with the shape of the instrument approach funnel, and extends for a distance of 1,000 metres, or 1,372 metres, from the end of the runway or planned extension, depending upon the level of movements at the aerodrome concerned. As originally conceived, a PSZ was 1,372 metres long, but such PSZs are now only established at the ends of major runways of busy aerodromes having an annual total of 45,000 or more specified movements. In January 1982 the DOT introduced a Standard PSZ 1,000 metres long. This reduction in length reflected the improved accident safety record experienced, and is applied at less busy aerodromes which have reached a minimum of 1,500 and have a potential for 2,500 specified movements a month. For PSZ purposes, a specified movement is taken to include all commercial and military movements, other than by light training types, but to exclude local pleasure, private, aero club and official flights as detailed in CAA Monthly Statistics. PSZ requirements bear no relation to the normal CAA aerodrome licensing process.

MET OBSERVATION PERIODS, BROADCAST FACILITIES, AIRCRAFT MOVEMENTS AND PSZ STATUS

AIRPORT	MET OBS PERIOD (mins)	MET BROADCAST FACILITIES	1994 AIR TRANSPORT MOVEMENTS	1994 TOTAL MOVEMENTS	CURRENT PSZ STATUS
HEATHROW	30	LM,SC,AT	411608	424557	L
GATWICK	30	LM,LN,AT	181879	191646	L
MANCHESTER	30	LM,LN,AT	145549	169908	L
ABERDEEN	30	SC,AT	79984	103056	L
GLASGOW	30	LM,SC,AT	75986	95482	L
BIRMINGHAM	30	LS,AT	71068	95278	S
EDINBURGH	30	SC,AT	61080	110265	L
STANSTED	30	LM,AT	57670	75261	L
JERSEY	30	LS,AT	49018	81308	-
GUERNSEY	30	AT	39850	61131	-
NEWCASTLE	30	LN,AT	37153	74507	S
EAST MIDLANDS	30	LN,AT	32954	61525	S
BELFAST INTL	30	SC,AT	32877	88325	-
BELFAST CITY	60	-	31938	40197	-
BRISTOL	30	LS,AT	26141	51598	S (NEW)
SUMBURGH	30	SC,AT	23326	27966	-
SOUTHAMPTON	30	LS,AT	23314	57876	S
LEEDS/BRADFORD	30	LN,AT	23002	49737	S (NEW)
LIVERPOOL	30	LN	20676	80223	S
ISLE OF MAN	30	LN	17516	39991	-
LUTON	30	LS,AT	17161	41588	S
LONDON CITY	30	-	16970	17341	VS
CARDIFF	30	LS,AT	16203	55742	S (NEW)
TEES-SIDE	30	LN	14489	55311	-
HUMBERSIDE	60	AT	12018	35633	-
ISLES OF SCILLY	60	-	10304	11425	-
EXETER	30	-	10198	51745	-
KIRKWALL	30	-	9198	11825	-
ALDERNEY	30	-	8559	13554	-
BOURNEMOUTH	30	LS,AT	8467	90025	S
NORWICH	30	LS	8128	34008	-
INVERNESS	30	SC	6988	23923	-
COVENTRY	60	-	6949	56683	-
BLACKPOOL	30	LN	6241	45877	-
PLYMOUTH	60	-	5453	26399	-
UNST	60	-	4782	6225	-
STORNOWAY	30	SC	3945	7072	-
WICK	30	-	3661	6007	-
CAMBRIDGE	60	-	3357	48290	-
SOUTHEND	30	LS,AT	3138	51223	S

KEY		PSZ
LM - LONDON VOLMET MAIN	SC - SCOTTISH VOLMET	L - 1372 m
LN - LONDON VOLMET NORTH	AT - ATIS	S - 1000 m
LS - LONDON VOLMET SOUTH		VS - 600 m

Permits to operate flights

With regard to the requirements to be met before an aircraft registered outside the United Kingdom (or, more recently, any member state of the European Union) can be used for cargo operations from an airport within the UK, the Air Navigation Order 1989, as amended, Article 88 paragraph 1 states:

"An aircraft registered in a Contracting State other than the United Kingdom, or in a foreign country, shall not take on board or discharge any passengers or cargo in the United Kingdom where valuable consideration is given or promised in respect of the carriage of such persons or cargo, except with the permission of the Secretary of State granted under this article to the operator or the charterer of the aircraft or to the Government of the country in which the aircraft is registered, and in accordance with any conditions to which such permission may be subject."

The procedure for applying for such a permit, to operate non-scheduled flights for commercial purposes, is outlined in the FAL section of the UK AIP, which section (paragraph 2.1.5.1.3) details the following information which is required to be submitted by the applicant for a Permit, normally giving five full working days notice for a series of two or more flights:

(a)   Name of operating company and address to which permit should be sent;
(b)   type of aircraft and nationality or registration marks;
(c)   date and estimated times of arrival at, and departure from, UK aerodromes;
(d)   place of embarkation or disembarkation abroad of freight;
(e)   nature of flight, eg freight;
(f)   name, address and business of charterer and the nature and amount of freight to be taken.

A note indicates that in considering applications, the DOT has regard to the conditions of such flights which are applicable to similar flights by UK operators.

The following documentary evidence requirements are also listed therein in respect of non-scheduled commercial operations:

(Para. 2.1.1.1.1) The Department of Transport will require evidence that the operating company is considered by the national authority of the State of registry of the aircraft to be operationally competent to undertake the type of flight concerned.
(ie holds a Certificate of Competency - referred to as an Air Operator's Certificate)

(Para. 2.1.1.2) The Department of Transport will require evidence that the aircraft to be operated is considered by the national authority of the State of registry of the aircraft to be airworthy.
(ie holds a current Certificate of Airworthiness)

(Para. 2.1.1.3) The Department of Transport will require evidence that the operating company of the aircraft has entered into adequate insurance arrangements in respect of the aircraft to be operated.
(ie holds a valid Certificate of Insurance)

Aerodrome Operating Minima - Notification Requirements

The following technical requirement is specified in the AIP, FAL section, detailing the procedures for applications to conduct Non-Scheduled Commercial Flights:

Para. 2.1.2.1 Application for permits for non-scheduled flights should include details of Aerodrome Operating Minima (see para. 1.13) for aircraft and aerodromes concerned where this information has not been previously notified to the CAA Flight Operations Inspectorate.

The following information is presented earlier in the FAL section regarding Aerodrome Operating Minima:

Para. 1.13.1 Articles 32 and 32A of the Air Navigation Order 1989 as amended, state that neither public nor non-public transport aircraft registered in a country other than the United Kingdom shall commence or continue an approach to landing at an aerodrome in the United Kingdom if the runway visual range for the relevant runway and approach aid at that aerodrome is less than the operator's specified minimum, unless:

(a) The aircraft is below decision height; and
(b) the specified visual reference has been established at decision height and is maintained.

Para 1.13.1.1 A copy of this prohibition, which must be included in instructions to crews, must be submitted to the Civil Aviation Authority with aerodrome operating minima.

Para 1.13.2 Each operator is asked to ensure that details of specific minima for Category 1 operations will reach the CAA at least 7 working days before the date(s) of the proposed flight(s) so that the operator can be advised of any amendments necessary to meet United Kingdom safety requirements.

Details of these minima are thus required to be forwarded to the Flight Operations Department of the CAA at Gatwick Airport in advance of the proposed flights.

The "specified visual reference" referred to above is intended to mean that reference as defined in the particular operator's Operations Manuals. This definition is included in the text of the relevant article in the Air Navigation Order, but is not reproduced in the AIP, FAL section.

COVENTRY, UK   EGBE   (11-1)

COVENTRY

N52 22.2 W001 28.7   088.5°/6.8 From HON 113.65

Elev **281'**   Var 05°W

*COVENTRY Ground **121.7** (Instructed by ATC)	
*Tower **124.8 119.25**	

WARNING: Colour coding of rwy lights on
starter extension rwy 23 shows red towards
05 apch and blue towards 23 apch.
Acft with wingspan in excess of 59'(18m)
will require marshalling.
Rwy shoulders liable to water-logging.
For Radar Minimums see Terminal Page E-51 etc.
Rwy 05 & 35 right-hand circuit.

Northern Airpark

Light Acft Park

Control Tower 333'

17 -175°

Eastern Light Acft Parking Area

Elev 281'

Grass Twy

Elev 265' 591'/180m Stopway

23 -232°

5299' 1615m

2674' 815m

Western Light Acft Parking Area

ARP

GRASS

South Apron

Helicopter Training Strip

Northern

305'93m Stopway

Elev 266'

F Grass G Twy

Elev 265'

98'30m Stopway

35 -355°

05 -052°

Feet	0	500	1000	1500	2000	2500	3000
Meters	0	200	400	600	800	1000	

ADDITIONAL RUNWAY INFORMATION

RWY		USABLE LENGTHS — LANDING BEYOND — Threshold	Glide Slope	TAKE-OFF	WIDTH
05 23	HIRL HIALS PAPI-L (angle 3.0°) RVR		4396' 1340m	❶	151' 46m
17 35					98' 30m

❶ Additional 689'(210m) are available for take-off if using starter extension. Total take-off length: 5988'(1825m). Starter extension not available to acft with under-slung engines.

❷ TAKE-OFF

	AIR CARRIER Rwy 05/23 HIRL	Rwy 17/35		
A	RVR *250m*	400m		
B	RVR *300m*			
C				
D	RVR *400m*	NOT APPLICABLE		

❷ UK auth: refer to TERMINAL page UNITED KINGDOM-1 etc.

CHANGES: Noise abatement proc transferred to 10-3.

RADAR LANDING MINIMUMS (cont'd)

LOCATION (Airport)	PROCEDURE TYPE, RWY	OCL/OCA (H) QNH (QFE)	LOWEST STRAIGHT-IN LANDING MINIMUMS	
			DA (H) MDA (H)	VISIBILITIES
UNITED KINGDOM (cont'd)				
CONINGSBY	PAR 08(2.5°)	#A: 222'(200')	222'(200')	1200m
		#B: 222'(200')	232'(210')	1200m
		#C: 222'(200')	242'(220')	1200m
		#D: 222'(200')	252'(230')	1200m
	PAR 08(3.0°)	#A: 222'(200')	252'(230')	1200m
		#B: 222'(200')	262'(240')	1200m
		#C: 222'(200')	272'(250')	1200m
		#D: 222'(200')	282'(260')	1200m
	PAR 26(2.5°)	#A: 225'(200')	225'(200')	R 720m V 800m
		#B: 225'(200')	235'(210')	R 720m V 800m
		#C: 225'(200')	245'(220')	R 720m V 800m
		#D: 225'(200')	255'(230')	R 720m V 800m
	PAR 26(3.0°)	#A: 225'(200')	255'(230')	R 720m V 800m
		#B: 225'(200')	265'(240')	R 720m V 800m
		#C: 225'(200')	275'(250')	R 720m V 800m
		#D: 225'(200')	285'(260')	R 720m V 800m
	PAR 08 Tmn 1 Azimuth only	#312'(290')	320'(298')	ABC: 1200m D: R 1500m V 1600m
	PAR 26 Tmn 0.5 Azimuth only	#345'(320')	350'(325')	ABC: 800m D: R 1500m V 1600m
	ASR 08 Tmn 1	#342'(320')	350'(328')	ABC: 1200m D: R 1500m V 1600m
	ASR 26 Tmn 1	#345'(320')	350'(325')	ABC: 800m D: R 1500m V 1600m

CAUTION: PAR 08 Azimuth only & ASR 08
           include stepdown fix at 3.0 NM. Do
           not descend below 410'(388')
           until advised by ATC.
           PAR 26 Azimuth only & ASR 26
           include stepdown fix at 3.0 NM. Do
           not descend below 420'(395')
           until advised by ATC.

\# RAF DH/MDA

COVENTRY*	SRA 05 Tmn 0.5	616'(350')	620'(354')	ABC: 1200m D: R 1500m V 1600m
	SRA 05 Tmn 1	616'(350')	620'(354')	ABC: 1200m D: R 1500m V 1600m
	SRA 05 Tmn 2	916'(650')	920'(654')	ABC: 1500m D: R 1500m V 1600m
	SRA 23 Tmn 0.5	635'(370')	640'(375')	ABCD: R 1500m V 1600m
	SRA 23 Tmn 1	635'(370')	640'(375')	ABCD: R 1500m V 1600m
	SRA 23 Tmn 2	915'(650')	920'(655')	ABCD: R 1500m V 1600m

SRA 05 Tmn 0.5: Pass FAF 4.5 NM at
           1670'(1404') or above.
SRA 05 Tmn 1: Pass FAF 5.0 NM at
           1820'(1554') or above.
SRA 05 Tmn 2: Pass FAF 5.0 NM at
           1820'(1554') or above.
SRA 23 Tmn 0.5: Pass FAF 4.5 NM at
           1670'(1405') or above.
SRA 23 Tmn 1: Pass FAF 5.0 NM at
           1820'(1555') or above.
SRA 23 Tmn 2: Pass FAF 5.0 NM at
           1820'(1555') or above.
All SRA: Descent Gradient 4.9%.

Aerodrome Operating Minima (AOM) requirements

The AOM for the conduct of an instrument approach to landing consists of three distinct parts, namely:

(a) a minimum height down to which the aircraft may be flown without visual reference to the landing runway or approach lighting;

(b) the precise visual reference required for landing, which must be attained by the end of the published approach procedure, and;

(c) a minimum visibility required to exist before commencing the approach procedure.

For a Precision Approach (eg ILS, MLS, PAR etc which have electronic glidepath guidance), the Decision Height (DH) is the height at which a missed approach must be initiated if the required visual reference to continue the approach has not been established.

For a non-precision approach (eg VOR, NDB, SRA etc where there is no electronic glidepath guidance), the Minimum Descent Height (MDH) is the height below which descent may not be made without the required visual reference.

The visual reference is defined in the AIP as "a view of the section of the runway and/or the approach area and/or their visual aids, which the pilot must see in sufficient time to assess whether or not a safe landing can be made from the type of approach being conducted."

The final element of AOM is the RVR. On reaching the DH/MDH after an instrument approach, the pilot must have a reasonable chance of being able to complete the approach to a manual landing by visual reference to ground features. The visibility required to achieve a landing will increase with a higher value of DH/MDH. An improved chance of landing will be obtained if high intensity lights are in use at the aerodrome. Therefore, for each DH/MDH, there is a corresponding RVR depending upon the type of approach and runway lighting in use. If the weather at the aerodrome includes an RVR worse than this minimum there is not a reasonable prospect of achieving a landing and consequently the pilot shall not commence or continue the approach to landing.

The Jeppesen Airway Manual defines the "Required Visual Reference" as follows: "When conducting an instrument approach procedure, the pilot shall not operate an aircraft below the prescribed MDH or continue an approach below the DH, unless the aircraft is in a position from which a normal approach to the runway of intended landing can be made and at least one of the following visual references is clearly visible to the pilot:

(a) Runway, runway markings, or runway lights.

(b) Approach lights.

(c) Threshold, threshold markings, or threshold lights.

(d) Touchdown zone, touchdown zone markings, or touchdown zone lights.

(e) Visual glide path indicator (such as VASI, PAPI).

(f) Any other feature which clearly identifies the landing surface."

AFTER TAKE-OFF

Air Cond & Press _____ SET
Start Switches _____ OFF
Gravel Protec Switch _____ OFF
Landing Gear _____ UP & OFF
Flaps _____ UP & OFF
Altimeters _____ 1013,2
Inboard Landing Lights (5000 FT) _____ OFF

DESCENT - APPROACH

Loose Objets _____ SECURE
Approach Briefing _____ REVIEWED
Anti-Ice _____ CLOSED/OPEN
Air Cond & Press _____ SET
Star Switches _____ LOW IGN
Gravel Proted Switch _____ AS REQUIRED
Altimeters & Instruments _____ SEı & CHECKE ı
EPR & IAS Bugs _____ CHECKED & SET
Inboard Landing Lights (5000 FT) _____ ON

LANDING

Recall _____ CHECKED
Speed Brake _____ ARMED, GREEN LIGHT
Landing Gear _____ DOWN 3 GREEN
Flaps _____ GREEN LIGHT
Altimeters _____ CHECKED

FLIGHT PHASE/CONDITION:	NON-HANDLING PILOT CALLS:
CLIMB AND DESCENT:	
1,000 feet above/below assigned altitude	"1,000 feet to level off"
DESCENT:	
5,000 feet MSL	"5,000 feet, landing lights on"
1,000 feet above initial approach altitude	"1,000 feet above initial
FINAL APPROACH:	
Final fix inbound (altimeter, instrument and flag crosscheck)	"At beacon, VOR, etc ____ feet," "altimeters and instruments crosschecked"
500 feet above field elevation (altimeter, instruments and flag crosscheck)	"500 feet above field," "altimeters and instruments crosschecked"
After 500 feet above field elevation	(Call out significant deviations from programmed airspeed, descent and instrument indications)
100 feet above minimums	"100 feet above minimums"
Minimum altitude (DH or MDH)	"Minimums, runway in sight" (or "no runway in sight")

AIR ALGERIE STANDARD ALTIMETER CHECKING PROCEDURES

APPENDIX S

7T-VEE FINAL FLIGHT PATH

Note: Speeds are Groundspeed calculated from Radar

9:45:20
... SET QFE 1013 DESCEND TO MAINTAIN HEIGHT 1500FT
AND TURN LEFT HEADING ZERO THREE ZERO

... ROGER THAT WAS -ER- ONTO RADAR HEADING NOW OF ZERO ONE ZERO

9:45:40
... ROGER THAT WAS -ER- ONTO RADAR HEADING NOW OF ZERO ONE ZERO

9:46:10
... CAN YOU TURN LEFT IMMEDIATELY NOW ONTO A HEADING OF ZERO ONE ZERO INITIALLY PLEASE

... ROGER AT THE MOMENT YOU'RE TRACKING ONE ZERO ZERO CAN YOU TURN LEFT TO ZERO ONE ZERO PLEASE

9:47:00
... CONTINUE THE LEFT TURN NOW ONTO A RADAR HEADING OF TWO SIX ZERO

9:44:50
... TURN LEFT NOW ONTO RADAR HEADING ZERO NINER ZERO

9:50:00
... TURN LEFT HEADING TWO FOUR ZERO.

9:50:20
... TURN FURTHER LEFT NOW TWO THREE ZERO THE HEADING ...

Height above Runway Elevation (ft)

Distance (East) from runway threshold (km)

Distance (North) from runway threshold (km)

S-1

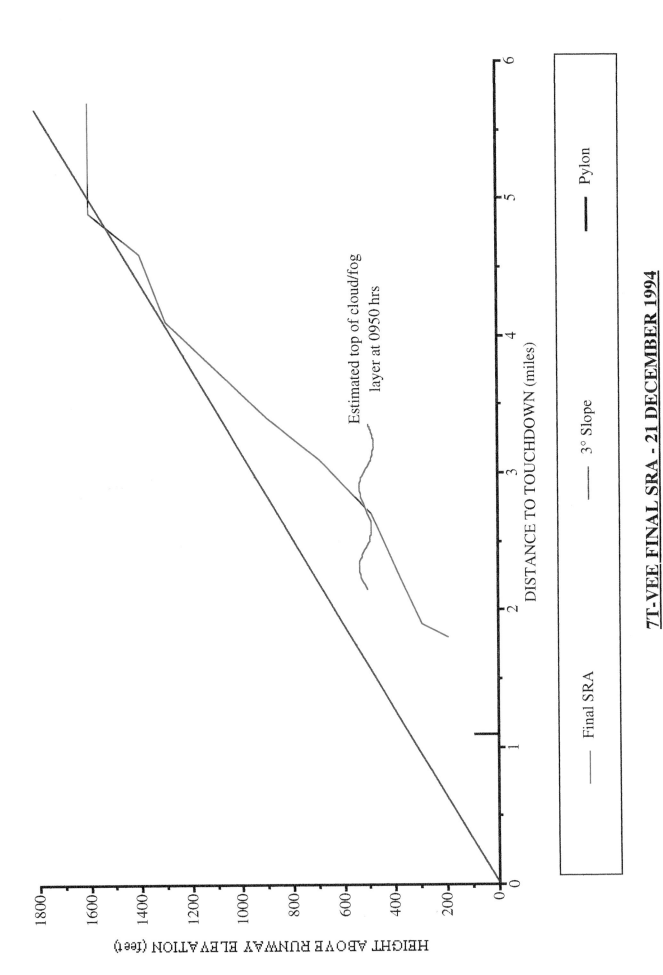

Estimated top of cloud/fog
layer at 0950 hrs

DISTANCE TO TOUCHDOWN (miles)

HEIGHT ABOVE RUNWAY ELEVATION (feet)

Final SRA   3° Slope   Pylon

7T-VEE FINAL SRA - 21 DECEMBER 1994

S - 2

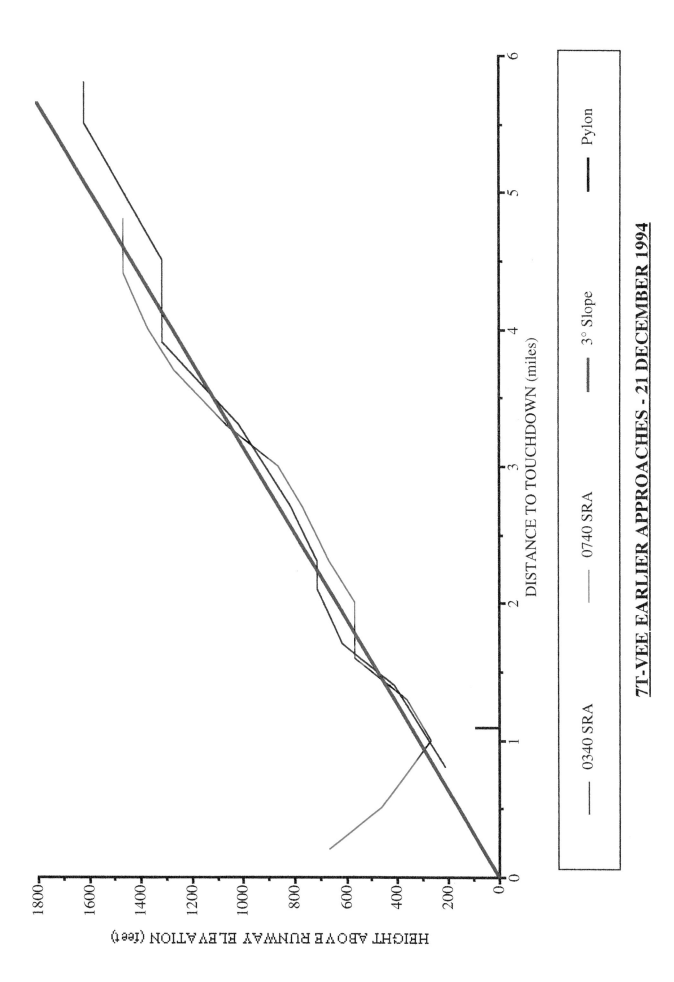

HEIGHT ABOVE RUNWAY ELEVATION (feet)

DISTANCE TO TOUCHDOWN (miles)

7T-VEE EARLIER APPROACHES - 21 DECEMBER 1994

0340 SRA   0740 SRA   3° Slope   Pylon

S - 3

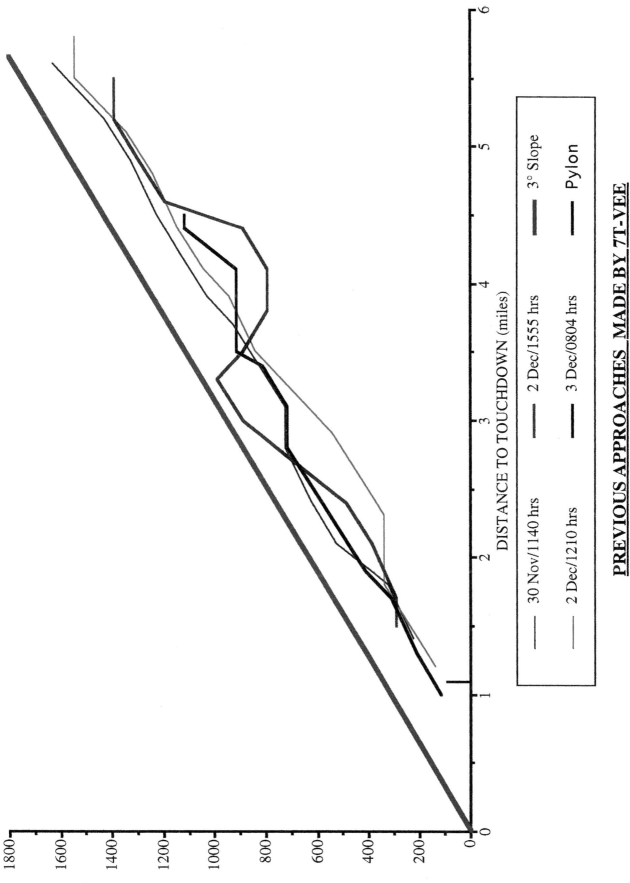

PREVIOUS APPROACHES MADE BY 7T-VEE

Attachment to Appendix E

	Phraseology
	Reply not received. If you read (ATSU callsign) turn left/right heading (three digits), I say again turn left/right heading (three digits).
	If you read (ATSU callsign) Squawk (code).
	Turn observed. I will continue to pass instructions.
	Squawk observed, I will continue to pass instructions.
Secondary Radar	Squawk (code).
	Confirm squawk (code).
	Recycle (mode) (code).
	Squawk Ident.
	Squawk Mayday.
	Squawk Standby.
	Squawk Charlie.
	Check altimeter setting and confirm level.
	Stop squawk Charlie. Wrong indication.
	Stop squawk Charlie.
	Stop squawk Alpha.
	Stop squawk.
	Verify your level.
	Confirm you are squawking assigned code (code assigned to the aircraft by air traffic control). *To verify that 7500 has been set intentionally.*
Radar Approaches	Vectoring for a surveillance radar approach; runway (designation).
	Vectoring for an ILS approach; runway (designation).
	Vectoring for a localiser only approach; runway (designation).
	This is a left/right hand circuit for runway (designation).
	Position (distance) miles (direction)* of (aerodrome).
	On left/right base leg (distance) miles (direction)* of (aerodrome).
	Direction is to be expressed as a cardinal or intermediate point of the compass.
	Closing final approach track from the left/right (distance) miles from touchdown.
	This turn will take you through (aid) (reason).
	Taking you through (aid) (reason).
	If you lose radio contact on this approach (instructions) and contact (ATSU callsign) on (frequency).
	This approach may be affected by clutter, advise you check the approach with ILS.
	This approach may be affected by clutter. Missed approach instructions will be passed in good time if necessary.
	(Type) approach not available due to (reason).

	Phraseology
ILS Approaches	Turn left/right heading (three digits), report established on the localiser.
	Closing the localiser from the left/right; report established.
	Descend on the ILS, QFE (pressure) millibars.
	Descend on the ILS, QNH (pressure) millibars, elevation (number) feet.
	(Distance) miles from touchdown.
	Height should be (number) feet.
	Report runway/approach lights in sight.
	Number (number) contact Tower (frequency).
	Contact (ATCU callsign) on (frequency) for final approach.
	After landing contact (ATCU callsign) on (frequency).
SURVEILLANCE RADAR APPROACHES	This will be a surveillance radar approach, terminating at (distance) mile from touchdown. Check your minima, step down fixes and missed approach point.
	Check wheels.
Azimuth information	Turn left/right (number) degrees, heading (three digits).
	Closing (final approach) track from the left/right.
	Heading of (three digits) is good.
	On track.
	Slightly left/right of track.
Descent information	Approaching (distance) miles from touchdown – commence descent now to maintain a (number) degree glidepath.
	(Distance) miles from touchdown – height should be (number) feet
	Do not reply to further instructions.
	Check minimum descent height.
Completion	Approach completed, out.
	Continue visually or go around (missed approach or further instructions).
Breaking off	Turn left/right (number) degrees, heading (three digits) climb to (number) feet (further instructions), acknowledge.
	Climb immediately, I say again climb immediately on heading (three digits) to altitude (number) feet (further instructions), acknowledge.

Printed in the United Kingdom for HMSO
Dd 301863 C5 1/96 341069 50/34275